THE**ADVOCATE**

GUIDE TO GAY MEN'S
HEALTH AND WELLNESS

THE ADVOCATE

GUIDE TO GAY MEN'S
HEALTH AND WELLNESS

FRANK SPINELLI, M.D.

alyson books
NEW YORK

MANUFACTURED IN THE UNITED STATES OF AMERICA

THIS TRADE PAPERBACK ORIGINAL IS PUBLISHED BY
ALYSON BOOKS
245 WEST 17TH STREET
NEW YORK, NY 10011

DISTRIBUTION IN THE UNITED KINGDOM BY
TURNAROUND PUBLISHER SERVICES LTD.
UNIT 3, OLYMPIA TRADING ESTATE
COBURG ROAD, WOOD GREEN
LONDON N22 6TZ ENGLAND

FIRST EDITION: JANUARY 2008

08   09   10   11   12   **a**   10   9   8   7   6   5   4   3   2   1

ISBN: 1-59350-040-8
ISBN-13: 978-1-59350-040-5

LIBRARY OF CONGRESS CATALOGING-IN-PUBLICATION DATA
ARE ON FILE.

DESIGN BY VICTOR MINGOVITS

To Eric,
who taught me that being nice is all you need,
and, despite everything, remember to laugh.

Contents

Preface

This book is intended for all gay men—especially those aged forty years and older—who want to take control of their lives in order to be healthier, and ultimately happier, individuals. The goal of this book is to alter and correct the public consciousness of gay people and to raise awareness about gay lifestyles.

In 2007, it is apparent that despite the increasing presence of gays in the media, being gay still harbors negative connotations. Celebrities and talk-show personalities still make statements denying their homosexuality, while many known gay personalities refuse to come out for fear of reprisal. The point is that gay men live with this burden of shame, and it affects how well we take care of ourselves. Homosexuality is a way of life. It is not a choice, and we are not defined by the sex act itself. Being gay is who we are.

Since the emergence of AIDS, the disease has become synonymous with gay health in general, and accurate, comprehensive information about gay sex has been either relegated to the back of bookstores or reduced to the brunt of tasteless jokes. As a clinician and primary-care health provider to many people, I realized that my role was complicated by the fact that gay health issues unrelated to HIV weren't being addressed. I found myself immersed in a new field, one that had not been taught to me formally in medical school or addressed in residency. The AIDS epidemic had necessitated a new attitude toward gays and lesbians, and the gay community was becoming motivated to open up to doctors with questions they had previously been too ashamed to ask.

All gay men should be empowered with a working knowledge of their health, sexuality, and lifestyle. Only this will enable them to make sound decisions to promote their wellness. Gay health requires that you follow a plan that will allow you to live your life to the fullest, without the constraints of homophobia. Since the average life expectancy for all men has increased, contemporary gay men need to educate themselves in order to maintain the same healthy bodies they had in their twenties and to disprove the tired myth that life ends at forty. There is a journey to be taken and to be lived, and with a vitality that will last you well into your seventies, eighties, and beyond.

Acknowledgments

This book could not have been possible without the help and guidance of so many people. First and foremost, I thank Robert Guinsler, my literary agent at Sterling Lord Literistics, along with everyone at Alyson Books, who shared my vision. Their support made this dream a reality. To my editor, Richard Fumosa, thank you for shepherding me through this project. You shaped and molded my ideas with great courage and gentle persuasion.

To all my medical mentors at Cabrini Medical Center, Dr. Roberto Aymat, Dr. Wilfredo Talavera, Dr. Jose Cortes, Dr. Michael Mullen, my best friend, Dr. Basit (P. J.) Qayyum, and the amazing Dr. Larry Higgins; you are the hardest-working heroes I have ever had the honor to learn from. To the best support team, I thank the ladies of the HIV Clinic: Jackie, Michelle, Daisy, Jackie, Gail, Emily, and my girl Sharon Nottage.

I thank God for giving me a wonderful family. Their support motivates me to do more every day: Mom, Dad, Josephine, Joe, Maria, Marc, and to all the little Ms—Matthew, Michael, Madeline, and Mitchell.

To all the knights of my round table who helped me usher in the most pivotal year of my life and the men I call my second family: Tony, Gabe, Mark, Miro, Michael, Fred, Ed, Tom, Luigi, Sean, and, most of all, Paul Cirone—this book is for you. A special thanks to Eric, Scott, Ron, and Gary. Over the years each one of you has lent your ear, your couch, and your completely unbiased opinion through some of the best and worst of times. I cherish our relationships.

To Joe, the kid, junior! Al, aka Magdo, and Ben, *Al Ahavot Shelanu.*

To Mark Peddigrew, Mark McVeigh, Peter Panaro, Dr. Laura Beauchamp, Michael Lucas, Eric Bean, Walter Armstrong, and Dave Schwing, thank you for all your input and valiant efforts. Lastly, to a great woman who has stuck by me despite hard times, my pseudo-wife, Wanda Martinez.

Molly, Ellie, Jada, and K. M., I love you.

Introduction:
A Doctor's Own Story

APPROACHING FORTY, I had the sudden realization that my life had not turned out exactly as planned. True, I had started my own private practice in Manhattan, and I was the clinical director of HIV services at Cabrini Medical Center by the time I was thirty eight, but something else was amiss. Though it could very well have been that I was single and that the threat of growing old by myself was frightening—as is normal—I thought otherwise. The question nagged me: What's missing in my life?

I began by asking my close friends if they shared similar feelings, and I was surprised to find that I was in good company. In fact, the more friends I asked, the more I found there to be a whole group of us who shared this similar and unexplainable feeling. I even began to ask my patients, especially those men my age or older, and once again I was surprised by the growing number of men who felt this void in their lives. What made it even more interesting was that we all came from different walks of life. Regardless of whether we were driven, successful, damaged, or complacent, being gay and approaching middle age had sparked a fear in all of us.

I wondered if this midlife crisis had anything to do with being gay—or did most adults struggle with this question? Was gayness even the issue?

Being gay is not something you are taught as a child. To the contrary, it is something that is strongly discouraged. Growing up the youngest of three children in a strict Italian-Catholic family, I was taught that being gay was a sin. My church went so far as to ban certain movies and television shows simply because they dealt with gay themes. As abiding Christians, my parents would not allow me to watch *Three's Company* or *Soap* because both of these shows had gay characters. It was my church's contention that if an impressionable child were exposed to the supposedly negative images of homosexuality, he might turn gay.

Even though, as a young boy, I knew on some level that I was gay, I, like most gay children, gravitated toward these shows, as if seeking knowledge—drawn to anything that had even the slightest homosexual undertone. Needless to say, I was devastated when my parents informed me that I could no longer watch *Three's Company.* I had to sneak to watch the show when my parents weren't home, and even when my father wasn't around, I could still hear his voice in the character of Mr. Roper, the homophobic landlord. His derogatory snipes and mocking gestures toward Jack were enough to make me cringe. Even then, I was afraid of being exposed as gay, and this led to much secrecy and isolation from my beloved friends and family.

Secrecy and isolation are closely related themes that recur in the lives of gay children. For instance, unlike other little boys, I was obsessed with the Bionic Woman, not the Six Million Dollar Man. A pleasure such as this was something I knew, instinctually, that I had to keep hidden in order to avoid ridicule. Being harassed as a child seems to create or augment issues of low self-esteem. Many gay men develop depression and social anxiety because of the years of torment they endured as children. Yet invisibility in childhood can become a means. It is easier to avoid ridicule if your tormentors just don't notice you. It becomes less important for the gay child to shine in the classroom, more important for him to hide. In my case, I stopped raising my hand in class, even when I knew the answer, and I crouched behind the student in front of me whenever the teacher looked for volunteers to erase the blackboard.

FACT: Gay and lesbian teens make up about 3 to 5 percent of the population, and certain health-related issues are specific to this growing population.

1.   They have higher suicide rates.
2.   There is an increased risk for mental health issues, especially depression.
3.   Gay teens practice high-risk sexual behavior and have higher rates of STDs and HIV.
4.   They tend to have poorer outcomes in school.
5.   They have higher rates of substance abuse and homelessness.

Self-mockery is a learned defense mechanism. Unfortunately, it is this same defense that leads to isolation in gay adults. It promotes ambivalence among gay men, so that when they become adults, they have a difficult time making healthy connections with each other. Many gay men complain that they feel depressed, dejected, and isolated, even within the gay community. This reality stands in stark contrast to the notion that, once a man comes out, the gay community will embrace him, and that all is solved. This concept of instantaneous and multilateral gay solidarity is commonly held—and false.

In 2000, I moved into Manhattan and found the gay bar scene to be a liberating and enthralling experience. I wasn't "out" at work. Despite the fact that the hospital was considered to be the epicenter of the AIDS crisis, the surgical program was not tolerant of homosexuals. I remained closeted at work and to my family, but slowly integrated myself into the gay social scene with the aid of my cousin Paul, who is seven years my junior and at the time was openly gay. His attitude toward being gay was devoid of the guilt that plagued me. His ability to "come out" to our family at the age of sixteen was inconceivable to me, because we both grew up in such similar households. The only major difference between us was our age, so it was this generation gap, I hopefully concluded, that was the reason we had such different views about being gay.

As a child, I was raised to go to school, get married, and take care of children—to become the proverbial breadwinner of the nuclear family. My cousin, on the other hand, did not share this burden.

Needless to say, it was not a complete surprise to my family when Paul "came out" at sixteen years old. What made me so envious of his "coming out" was that he did it with no remorse or any sense of apology. Even as my aunt smacked her head repeatedly against the living room wall, I could see in Paul's eyes that he did not think that he was to blame. He was gay, and that was just the way it was. It would take me twelve more years to get up enough courage to follow suit.

After I returned from medical school, Paul served as my gay mentor and showed me the ropes of the gay bar scene, even though I still held onto the stupid notion that I might be heterosexual. He knew I was struggling, but he helped me to come out, and for that, I am forever indebted to him. I officially "came out" at the ripe old age of twenty-eight. By then, I was in my first year of medical residency and had started dating a handsome young salesman named Jack, who later broke my heart. At this time, it was my contention that as a mature adult, secure in my profession and relationship, the news of my sexuality would not be delivered from an impressionable young man brainwashed by years of *Three's Company*, but from a mature young doctor.

My plan was to tell my parents on my next visit back home to Staten Island. It was customary for them to drive me back to Manhattan after a visit. On this occasion, I offered to drive myself. I didn't want the news to startle my father into an accident. As we passed over the Verrazano Narrows Bridge, I locked all the car doors so that neither parent could escape. As we passed the first of the two powder-blue towers, I looked into the rearview mirror as my old hometown faded away. It was time. Without pause, I calmly and succinctly revealed to them that I was gay. There was a long moment of silence. I could not bear to look at my parents as so I stared at the road ahead of me. Breathless with anticipation of their response, I felt a weight had been lifted. For better or for worse, I had been freed from this guilt, and now it was in their hands and hearts, to make their own peace with it.

My father was silent, which was not unusual. My mother and I talked calmly, which was unusual, but all in all we were communicating. Looking back now, I know that had I not been an adult, they might not have accepted my coming out as easily as they did. That is not to say that they were happy. They were very concerned and somewhat disappointed, but that was understandable. What did these two Italian immigrants know about gays, other then the negative images that had been reinforced by the media and their church? To my parents, being gay meant getting AIDS and burning in hell. I was their only son. I was supposed to get married and have their grandchildren. How could I blame them for being disappointed? The remorse over not living up to my parents' expectations was something I had to struggle with for years.

Guilt is another recurring theme in the lives of gay men. Even though I am older now and have come to terms with my sexuality through therapy, I still feel occasional pangs of guilt. It is my personal and professional experience that the above-described combination of factors, including guilt and disappointment, promotes internalized homophobia. This underlying self-hatred hinders adult gay men as they try to take authority over their own lives.

The conversion from heterosexual identification to a homosexual identification is a complicated process. Coming to terms with your sexuality can take years, and for some, staying in the closet is a self-imposed and continual prison. There are many men, even in this day and age, who insist on living a lie. These men lead double lives. They marry women to keep up the pretense of a "normal," heterosexual life while they discreetly have sex with men. In the African-American community, there is the notion of life on the "down low," whereby African-American men, who consider themselves straight, take part in sexual activity with other men.

Those men who do come out must endure the complex process of re-entering normal society. The out male must learn to accept his new identity and must decide how he will deal with the day-to-day interactions with his family, friends, and co-workers. He must also unlearn much of what society has taught him. Otherwise, these daily challenges to his new identity will eventually lead to issues with shame, depression, and isolation. I refer to this process as "re-parenting."

A gay child, unlike other minorities, does not have the luxury of identifying with his or her family as a member of their minority.

Once a child discovers that he is different, it is unlikely that he will seek help from his parents unless he has been raised in a house that has shown acceptance to the gay community. So how do gay men learn to "re-parent" themselves? Therapy is an important step. But what if you can't afford therapy?

Currently, there are lesbian, gay, bisexual, and transgender (LGBT) centers all across the United States. These centers are easy to locate through the Internet and local directory assistance. LGBT centers accommodate gays and lesbians with low incomes and can even facilitate financial assistance.

LGBT centers can be found in most major cities and provide:

1. Substance abuse counseling and treatment
2. Mental health treatment

3. HIV testing and STD screening
4. General medical help

I am very proud to be a part of the Cabrini Medical Center LGBT Initiative. Not only do we offer all of the above services but we also provide a safe haven for gay men who feel that they have nowhere else to go. As a physician, after having interviewed hundreds of gay men, I find it interesting how similar the early developmental years of our lives have been. Growing up in the closet promotes alienation and disappointment. Later, this translates into depression, loneliness, and discontent. To fill this void, many gay men turn to drugs, alcohol, and sex.

Coming out often pushes men into a kind of "gay puberty," or "gay adolescence." This second adolescence may be filled with the traditional rites of passage: parties, drinking, and sex. Suddenly, men may become body conscious and feel the peer pressure to join a gym. They wear tight T-shirts to show off their new muscles, drink in crowded bars pressed up against other men, and dance alongside them in clubs until dawn. Along with all the excessiveness of the gay party scene comes the realization that this gay subculture knows no class division. The wealthy party right alongside the poor, and as long as you are young and beautiful, life is fabulous. Men often feel a strong desire to be part of this world. Coming out often correlates as the first true time a gay man takes up his own personal authority. He is no longer his parents' son or what they wanted him to be. He is his own person.

Psychologically, the conversion from straight to gay is confusing. Many men are so fearful of this conversion that they refuse to accept it and thus commit to a life in the closet. For most, it takes years to fully come to grips with their sexuality; for others, becoming gay is something they accept almost right away.

My private practice is located in Chelsea, which is an area of Manhattan that has a high concentration of gay men. I am openly gay, and although my patients know this, there is still a certain degree of shyness when I try to get them to discuss their sexual history. Obviously, not everyone is comfortable with talking about sex, but I feel that a man's sexual history is just as important a part of a patient's history as any other. I try my best to approach the matter as someone who is nonjudgmental. My feeling is that I would rather know the truth so that I am better able to serve my patients. The majority of my patients appreciate this approach, although it takes a period of adjustment. A certain level of trust has to be established.

For example, I had a patient named John who was fifty years old. On his initial visit, I asked if he was sexually active. He confirmed that he was, and I followed up this question with *Do you engage in sexual activity with women or men?* I feel it is more appropriate not to label patients as gay or straight. Labeling patients can be perceived as judging them. John was hesitant to answer, although he did confirm that he engaged in sexual activity with men. I sensed his timidity and concluded his sexual history by making sure he practiced safe sex by using condoms.

On John's follow-up visit two weeks later, he appeared guarded. As we sat down to discuss his labs, he interrupted me by saying he had something urgent to discuss. John informed me that he was angry when I asked him about sex—his sexual practices were a private matter, he said, and he did not want this information in his chart. I reassured John that under New York State law, his chart was confidential and any information in it could not be divulged with out his written consent. John seemed more at ease after our discussion, but I later found myself thinking that clearly, John was not comfortable with his sexuality, and harbored a certain amount of internalized homophobia.

Internalized homophobia is a source of conflict that can translate into shame for many gay men: shame about loving the same sex and shame over wanting sexual pleasures that are regarded as unnatural. Shame is one of the reasons why gay men find it difficult to talk about sex. It is so important that all gay men understand the fundamental facts about gay sex because, by and large, many of the daily problems for which I treat gay men are predicated upon the fact that they are ignorant about sexual issues. This is completely understandable because gay men do not learn about the birds and the bees from their fathers—they learn on their own, talking with their gay friends, or from watching pornography.

The sexual practices of gay men lend themselves to certain ailments that will be covered in this book. An open line of communication must be established between patients and their doctors. That is why it is paramount that all gay men find a doctor who is gay, or at least one who is sensitive to gay issues.

THE ADVOCATE

GUIDE TO GAY MEN'S
HEALTH AND WELLNESS

PART I

Gay
Health
Care

CHAPTER 1

Coming Out to Your Doctor

APPROACHING FORTY can be a pivotal moment in the life of gay men. It is a time when many men take a long hard look in the bathroom mirror. Their inspection may reveal that once soft, brown, wavy hair has become overpopulated by coarse, wiry, gray ones, and that dark circles of stress under the eyes, which normally vanish with some sleep, have now been tarnished with time. Further inspection—a complete 360-degree view of oneself (which is recommended periodically so you are not suddenly taken aback one day when you catch sight of your backside in a department store dressing room as you try on a new bathing suit)—may reveal that age is catching up to you. Gravity has convinced your waistline to soften, and the dreaded fear of back fat has begun to rear its ugly head. Is there anything you can do?

The two most useful promises you need to make to yourself at forty are these:

Pay closer attention to your diet and exercise routine.

Start a strict daily facial regimen.

Parenthetically, the changes going on with the outside of your body may ignite a fuse of fear that something even more insidious is going on inside, waiting to explode. The question becomes: "How healthy am I?" (The only way to know is to seek a doctor's opinion.) Then, as a gay man you shoud think, "What should I look for in a doctor?" or more important, "Should I find a gay doctor?" (The answer is yes!)

Historically, homosexuals have avoided health care or remained closeted to their health-care provider due to the threat of homophobia. Doctors are notorious for being judgmental toward their homosexual patients, simply because they are uncomfortable with the gay lifestyle themselves. Many straight doctors I've talked to make the same errors that I made initially as a young general practitioner—they unknowingly label their patients and try to categorize them. We all do this in our everyday lives. It makes us feel comfortable.

Questions involving sexuality may be regarded as an invasion of one's privacy, especially when asked on the initial visit. Asking a patient, point blank, if they are gay or straight creates an immediate barrier between the patient and the doctor. Regardless of their sexual orientation, forcing someone to "label" themselves can be perceived by the patient as a form of judgment. To corner a patient in such a manner can make them feel vulnerable. Dr. Lawrence Higgins, one of the best medical mentors I had the privilege of training with, once warned me about labeling patients. He suggested that the more appropriate way to elicit a sexual history from a patient was to first ask them, "How frequently they have sex with women and men?" A November 2006 article published in the *Journal of the American Medical Association* suggested that doctors should ask their patients the question, "Do you have sex with men, women, or both?" Simple adjustments such as these are far less confrontational to patients and open the door to discussion. This approach also suggests that the doctor is nonbiased and understands that people are sexually active in different ways. Included are bisexuals as well as a subgroup of heterosexual men who sometimes engage in sexual activity with other men who do not consider themselves bisexual. Sexual desire is particularly important to discuss, especially for men who are not comfortable discussing sexual acts as they pertain to an identity. For example there is a subgroup of African-American men who consider themselves heterosexual yet they participate in sexual activity with other men. This concept was brilliantly realized in J. L. King's book, *On the Down Low: A Journey into the Lives of "Straight" Black Men Who Sleep with Men.* The importance of these issues is not to exclude men by categorizing them as homosexual, but rather to adopt the more appropriate term, *MSM*, or *men who have sex with men.*

Some men desperately want to come out to their doctors. It may be a good idea in such cases if the doctor asks if they have ever felt an attraction to another man in order to provoke a conversation. It is important to keep an open mind because men come out at all ages and some may even be married and have children. This can be an even more difficult process for men who are already a member of a minority group—racial or religious. Imagine the impact of being both a sexual and a racial/religious minority in your country. Finding your identity as a gay

I AM REMINDED OF one Friday morning when two elderly gentlemen came into my office. One was a new patient and the other was introduced to me as his "friend." Usually, I do not see patients with their "friends" present, but the patient was clearly nervous. As we talked about his medical history, I asked my patient if he was single, married, or partnered. The patient told me he was "*not* married." He and his "friend" then exchanged knowing glances. I was suspicious but knew no additional information would be offered, so I continued, "Well, then, do you live alone?" Begrudgingly he replied, "I live with my friend." Eventually he confessed and told me that they had been living together for forty years and that their relationship was an intimate one. This information was produced after much interrogation, but it was not revealed until I was forced to press the issue. Afterward I queried, "Why didn't you just come right out and tell me?" They replied, "Because we weren't sure about you." These two gay men had been in a forty-year relationship and, despite the fact that they were sitting in an HIV clinic opposite a male doctor, they still felt compelled to hide their sexuality until they felt more at ease with me. This encounter taught me two valuable lessons:

1. Never to assume that my patients know I'm gay
2. The power of the closet still exists

If anything, this experience reinforced my belief that finding a gay doctor or one who is gay friendly is paramount to your health as a gay man. I could not imagine life otherwise.

Another example comes courtesy of a friend, Greg, who went to see a doctor about a lump that developed under his nipple. He was worried that it might be cancer; however, after his initial consultation, Greg was more concerned with his new doctor's behavior than with whether or not he had cancer.

During the history portion of the visit, Greg told his doctor that he was gay, and he immediately noticed a change in his doctor's demeanor. The man became nervous and dismissive, and Greg clearly felt that the doctor was uncomfortable with his homosexuality. After the consultation, Greg followed his doctor's orders and returned in one week. They reviewed the results of Greg's tests, and interestingly, he found that his doctor had ordered a whole slew of tests for sexually transmitted diseases and HIV, despite the fact that Greg said he was in a long-term, monogamous relationship. Greg was quite embarrassed and wondered if his doctor ordered these tests routinely on all his patients or specifically for Greg because he had identified himself as gay? I gave the doctor the benefit of the doubt, but I was suspicious myself. Was Greg's new doctor acting in a way to suggest that gay men are more promiscuous than the general population, when Greg had explicitly told him that he was in a long-term relationship? Regardless of the answer, it was obvious that there was a breach in trust. Greg had not been made to feel like he was an active participant in his care plan. His doctor had acted without including Greg, and this, in turn, made him feel uncomfortable.

Final outcome: He had the lump removed by a good surgeon, but afterward he found himself a gay primary care doctor whom I recommended.

man is complicated enough; having to integrate this with your existing persona involves quite a bit of ingenuity.

It is difficult to quantify the number of gay men who live in the United States. Several studies have attempted to estimate the prevalence of homosexuals. In 1994, E. O. Laumann found that 2.8 percent of all men described themselves as gay, whereas in the same report revealed that 9.1 percent described themselves as having had a same-sex sexual encounter. This statistic reiterates the fact that there are men who do not identify themselves as gay for many reasons. While some men will eventually identify themselves as gay, more do not because of internalized homophobia, bisexuality, and racial prejudice. This has forced clinicians into creating the aforementioned term, MSM.

In light of these issues, it may be best for doctors to stop asking all patients if they are "single, married, or divorced," as these categories are too narrow. Many gay patients, even those who are in a long-term relationship, do not consider themselves "married." Marriage is a legal entity that does not exist for homosexuals, many of whom say that they are single, despite the fact that they are in a long-term relationship. *Partnered* is a more suitable word because it is important for doctors to come across as gay friendly, even if you are a gay doctor.

One of the most important aspects of a great doctor-patient relationship is trust. A physician should always encourage patients to tell the truth: "A doctor is not your mother and not the police. He or she is there to help you, and without the truth, a doctor cannot help you." Most patients would feel comfortable with this approach, and it makes a doctor-patient relationship a bit easier.

Linked with the idea of trust is honesty, which is why you should come out to your doctor. All gay men are urged to do so. Some people argue that their sexuality is something that they feel they do not need to disclose to their doctor, but this is nonsense. Your sexuality and your lifestyle are important contributing factors to your health. It is vital that your doctor understands everything there is to know about you. Coming out to your doctor should not be burdened by shame, and if your doctor is not comfortable with treating homosexuals, then you should find yourself a new doctor.

CHAPTER 2

Health Care and Gay Men in the United States

IF YOU HAPPEN to be one of the privileged Americans who have private health insurance, then consider yourself lucky. According to the U.S. Census Bureau, approximately 85 percent of Americans have some form of health insurance and 60 percent obtain insurance through their employment. Having health care in America is about as vital as having a place to go home to at night; however, uninsured Americans make up over 16 percent of the population, or over 48 million people. This number rose substantially between 2003 and 2006, and even more worrisome is that the percentage of people with employment-based health insurance has dropped from 70 percent in 1987 to 59 percent in 2004. This issue is particularly problematic for gays, as the ratio of uninsured individuals is 2:1 compared to heterosexuals. Even with the rising number of domestic partnership benefits, most homosexuals are excluded from the same benefits afforded to married heterosexual couples. Additionally, even with domestic partnership benefits, some gay men still refuse to come out at work due to the threat of homophobia. Complicating matters further is the issue of insurance carriers delaying benefits or refusing to take on individuals with preexisting conditions such as HIV. The dilemma of health care and gay men is complex and disheartening for all these reasons and more. The American Cancer Society recently published data showing that since gay men are less likely to have health insurance and seek out medical attention for reasons concerning homophobia, they are more likely to suffer from lung cancer, especially since gay men tend to smoke more (41 percent) than the general population. Incidentally, smoking is known to accelerate the progression of HIV disease.

As we age, our dependence on health care increases and the rising costs of medicine, hospitalizations, and doctors' fees can make choosing an insurance carrier a difficult decision. Businesses that provide health insurance often offer a choice. The options may vary from indemnity plans to managed care plans and the difference between the two is as follows:

Managed care options require you to choose a doctor who participates in their plan. Plans such as HMOs (health maintenance organization) are prepaid health plans in which you pay a monthly premium and the HMO covers your office visits, hospital stays, emergency care, surgery, checkups, lab tests, X-rays, and therapy. You also pay a predetermined co-payment for each service and must choose a primary-care physician who coordinates all of your care and makes referrals to any specialists you might need. In an HMO, you must use the doctors, hospitals, and clinics that participate in your plan's network. PPOs (preferred provider organization) are a network of health-care providers in which a health insurer has negotiated contracts for its members to receive health services at discounted costs. Health-care decisions generally remain with the patient as he selects physicians, and patients are given incentives to select providers within the PPO network.

Indemnity plans consist of picking your own doctor and then paying him up front. Then after submitting the claim, you will be reimbursed by the insurance company.

The Consolidated Omnibus Budget Reconciliation Act of 1985, commonly referred to as COBRA, requires group health plans to be offered to you for eighteen months after you leave your job. Longer durations are available under certain circumstances if you wish to continue coverage; however, you must pay the entire premium, plus an administration charge.

Men over the age of 65 are all automatically covered by Medicare in the United States. This is a federally sponsored health insurance program for hospital and medical coverage. Medicaid is a joint federal-state health insurance program that is run by individual states and covers low-income and disabled people. Men with HIV are eligible for the AIDS Drug Assistance Program, or ADAP, for people with limited income and assets. ADAP is unique to each state and they decide which medications will be included in its formulary and how those medications will be distributed. Criteria for enrollment are established by each individual state, but all such enrollments require a positive HIV test.

ADAP pays for many HIV prescription drugs, while ADAP-Plus covers the cost for doctor visits and labs. It is important for you to know that ADAP does not cover inpatient hospitalizations or any bills incurred before ADAP was instituted. Also emergency room visits are not covered by ADAP and many prescription drugs, not related to HIV, are also not covered by ADAP. Treatment for alcoholism and drug addiction, physical rehabilitation services such as physical therapy and speech therapy, counseling related to HIV testing, and case management are also not covered.

FIVE MEDICAL LEGAL ISSUES EVERY GAY MAN SHOULD CONSIDER

This section is meant to be informative only. Individual situations are likely to vary. I strongly urge you to contact and obtain legal advice and assistance from an attorney when considering any of these options. It is important to note that, depending on the state in which you reside, laws may vary, particularly with respect to civil unions, marriage, and domestic partnerships as they relate to gay people.

1. *DNR, or Do Not Resuscitute order.* This is a document that provides your family and health-care providers with instructions to not place you on artificial life support in case of heart or lung failure, especially if you are unable to make a

conscious decision at the time. The DNR is a written order from a doctor indicating that you do not wish to be "coded." Such an order may be instituted on the basis of an advanced directive from a person that is entitled to make decisions on your behalf, such as a health care proxy. In situations where you do not have a health-care proxy then either your spouse, partner, or your closest living relative gets to make these decisions on your behalf as determined by the applicable state law. In the United States, a valid DNR will ensure that cardiopulmonary resuscitation, and advanced life support will not be performed. To ensure that your DNR is honored, be sure to instruct your partner, family, friends, and doctors of your wishes. A DNR order must be specific and the terms should be laid out. For example, some individuals are specific about not wanting CPR yet will allow mechanical ventilation, feeding tubes, and pain management. In any case, discuss the specifics with your doctor.

2. *A living will.* A type of advanced healthcare directive often accompanied by a specific type of power of attorney or health-care proxy. Generally speaking it has to be witnessed and notarized. A living will covers specific instructions as it pertains to your treatment, even if you are unable to give an informed consent at the time due to incapacity. A DNR can be part of a living will. A living will is a statement of your wishes regarding end-of-life care. Unlike a health-care proxy, a living will does not empower another person to make important medical decisions if you are incapacitated. Instead, a living will gives direction to your healthcare provider or representative

regarding what measures you want taken to prolong life and can serve to help assure that your wishes are being followed.

It is recommended that you obtain both a health-care proxy and a living will to ensure that your preferences about medical treatment are honored. Remember once again this is crucial. Recall the recent case involving Theresa Schiavo, who was declared brain dead but remained alive with the help of a feeding tube. Her parents battled with her legal husband about maintaining her life with the aid of this feeding tube, despite the fact that her legally recognized husband thought otherwise. In the case of a gay husband the wishes of the parent would likely be upheld.

3. *A health-care proxy.* Another legal document used in the United States in order to empower someone you have appointed to make health-care decisions in the event that you are incapable of doing so. The proxy cannot make a health-care decision as long as you, the primary individual, have the capacity to do so. They allow the patient's wishes to be followed when he is incapable of communicating them. Unless you have a documented proxy, decisions made on your behalf will be deferred to your next of kin, not your partner.

4. *A power of attorney.* They can be general or specific. Essentially, it is an individual appointed by you who will act on your behalf in legal and financial decisions should you be unable to do so. This will allow a designated person to sign certain documents on your behalf and make informed decisions depending upon what you have authorized this person to do.

5. *A last will and testament.* In the event of your death, a last will and testament will ensure proper distribution of your money, assets, and property to the desired individuals. Without a written will, your estate will be distributed to your legally recognized family. In the event of one of the deaths of a partnership, in the absence of a valid last will and testament, money, assets, and property would go to the closet legally recognized living relative, not his partner.

CHAPTER 3

A Guide to the Gay Man's Physical Exam

GENERALLY, ALL PATIENTS should be screened annually for heart disease and cancer. Routine annual physicals should always include height and weight assessments, blood pressure readings, and temperature measurements as a way to monitor patients over time, but also to hint at impending disease states. High blood pressure is usually a silent disease and, if left untreated, may lead to issues with heart and kidney disease. Loss of height may indicate osteoporosis, while weight gain can mean fluid retention but can also indicate heart, liver, or kidney disease. On the other hand, weight loss can be a consequence of infection or cancer. Likewise, baseline blood work should include checking cholesterol (high levels are a contributor to coronary artery disease), sugar (an indicator for diabetes), and baseline electrolytes, urine analysis, and complete blood counts to assess heart and kidney health.

For men over age forty, it is recommended that a digital rectal exam be performed to palpate the prostate. This will test not only for prostate cancer but for fecal occult blood (FOB), which is a screening tool for colon cancer. In addition to the digital rectal exam, a prostate specific antigen, or PSA (a blood test that aids in screening for prostate cancer), is also highly recommended. After age fifty, a screening called a colonoscopy is important to assess the entire colon for the possibility of cancer, polyps, or other abnormalities.

The annual physical exam is taught as a universal modality in medical schools. Since there are certain risk factors that pertain specifically to the gay community, this discussion will focus on aspects of the physical exam that are critical for gay men.

THE DIGITAL RECTAL EXAM

This is a useful diagnostic tool to screen for both colon and prostate cancers. In my experience, it is also the part of the examination that the patient most dreads—but it is necessary.

According to the American Cancer Society, colorectal cancer screening guidelines for both men and women should begin at age fifty with one of the following:

1. Yearly stool blood test (FOBT) or fecal immuno-chemical test (FIT)
2. Flexible sigmoidoscopy every five years
3. Yearly stool blood test *plus* flexible sigmoidoscopy every five years

For the stool blood test, the take-home, multiple-sample method should be used.

(Of the first three options, the American Cancer Society prefers the third option, that is, FOBT or FIT every year plus flexible sigmoidoscopy every five years.)

Or you may have:

4. Double contrast barium enema every five years
5. Colonoscopy every ten years

A colonoscopy is recommended for all men over the age of fifty—or earlier (age forty) for high-risk patients like African-Americans or men with a family history of prostate or colon cancer. Gay men should have a rectal exam beginning at age forty. After the exam is performed, a Guaiac Card is used to test for microscopic blood, also called the fecal occult blood test (FOBT), which is a screening test for colon cancer.

Colorectal cancer is the third most prevalent cancer found in men and women in this country. The American Cancer Society estimates that there were about 106,680 new cases of colon cancer and 41,930 new cases of rectal cancer in 2006 in the United States alone. Combined, they will cause about 55,170 deaths. The death rate from colorectal cancer has steadily decreased over the past fifteen years, thanks, in part, to proper colorectal cancer screening, like the FOBT. Even with these startling numbers, the good news is that colorectal cancer can be cured if found early.

However, despite its utility, the FOBT misses one in three cancers. That is why a positive FOBT should be followed up with a flexible sigmoidoscopy. This test, usually performed by a gastroenterologist, uses a fiberoptic tube that is inserted into the rectum to assess the lower colon. Polyps or any suspicious growth should be biopsied.

Dr. Frank's Quick Facts

> Digital rectal exam after age forty to screen for prostate cancer and colon cancer using FOB
> Positive FOB should be followed up with flexible sigmoidoscopy
> Screening colonoscopy at age fifty

A colonoscopy, on the other hand, is a much more thorough examination of the entire colon. Patients must be prepped the night before with a powerful laxative to clean out the colon offering the doctor better visibility. It is performed in a hospital or a doctor's office, and the patient is given sedation during the procedure. Once again, polyps and suspicious lesions should be biopsied. If any polyps or suspicious lesion are detected, the procedure can be repeated the following year. If the colonoscopy is normal, it should be repeated every three to five years thereafter.

THE MALE PAP SMEAR

In a recent study in *The New England Journal of Medicine*, gay and bisexual men were found to have a significantly higher risk for developing anal cancer, over thirty-five times greater than the general population. HIV-positive men were estimated to be eighty times more likely to get it. Although anal cancer accounts for less than 5 percent of all digestive and intestinal tract cancers, the rates have increased 160 percent over a thirty-year period. Gay African-American men have the sharpest increase and the lowest survival rates. Interestingly, anal cancer in gay men is as common as cervical cancer was in women before the use of the Pap smear, the test that screens for precancerous lesions on the cervix. Both types of cancer are caused by the human papillomavirus (HPV), which also causes anal and genital warts. HPV is one of the most common STDs in the world. Fortunately, anal cancer is highly preventable and treatable if caught in time.

There are more then one hundred different subtypes of HPV, and some are the source of common warts as seen on the hands and feet. HPV affects approximately 65 percent of HIV-negative gay men, and nearly 95 percent of HIV-positive gay men carry HPV in their anal canals. Most do not even know they have it. Subtypes 6 and 11 cause 90 percent of genital warts, while subtypes 16 and 18 are far more dangerous because of their precancerous potential.

The lining of the anal canal, once infected with HPV, can reproduce uncontrollably if left untreated. In most cases, the immune system clears the infection naturally, but in a small number of cases, usually over many years, HPV can cause changes in the cells of the anus and rectum that can lead to cancer. The Pap smear is something that should be offered to all gay men. In March 2007, the New York State Department of Health AIDS Institute, in collaboration with the Johns Hopkins Division of Infectious Diseases, issued a recommendation concerning anal Pap smear.

Clinicians should perform anal Pap tests at baseline and annually in the following populations:

1. Men who have sex with men
2. Any patient with a history of anal or genital warts

ONCE I HAD A patient with an anal wart that was the size of a grape, sticking out of his anus. He admitted that he had had it for months, and I was shocked that he ignored it for so long. Genital warts usually start out as small lesions that have a cauliflowerlike appearance. They can spread and grow, but to expand to the size of a grape takes a while. I could not even begin to explain why this patient chose to ignore it for so long. The wart was so large that it had to be removed surgically. What's the point here? Men should not ignore bumps or lesions on the penis, scrotum, or anus. The pathology after his surgery was HPV. Since then, he has routine anal Pap smears to check for recurrence.

Clinicians should refer patients with abnormal anal Pap test findings for high-resolution anoscopy and/or examination with biopsy. Like cervical cancer, invasive squamous cell cancers of the anal canal are associated with certain types of HPV infection, most notably, HPV-16 and HPV-18. Although this is a new practice that may not be routinely available, screening for cellular dysplasia is recommended, particularly in persons at high risk for infection with papilloma viruses.

Another good example of the ubiquitous nature of HPV concerns Mark, a patient I referred to a gastroenterologist for a colonoscopy after developing rectal bleeding. The results yielded several HPV warts in his rectum. This was much to Mark's surprise as he swore to me that he had been with the same person sexually for two years and therefore was unable to conceive how he had contracted this virus. I calmly reminded him that the virus could remain dormant for many years, especially if left untreated. Then he remembered a former partner from ten years earlier who had been diagnosed with HPV on his tongue. Mark had most likely contracted the virus through oral-anal contact. Unbeknownst to him, he had harbored those warts for the past ten years. The warts were removed during the colonoscopy and Mark was instructed to follow up in one year. Needless to say, all his other boyfriends from the past ten years had to be notified.

There are various ways to treat genital and anal warts depending on the size and location. Topical medications, like podofilox, which burns warts, can also burn the surrounding skin, so it is recommended that patients apply

Vaseline or zinc oxide around the wart to protect healthy skin. Imiquimod, which goes by the brand name Aldara, another topical cream, is also directly applied to the wart, and acts to diminish it as well, but is reserved for only minor warts. Cryotherapy with liquid nitrogen freezes warts and is done in a doctor's office; likewise, electrodesiccation, in which warts are burned off with an electric cautery, is another treatment. Other treatment options include topical use of trichloroacetic acid or bichloroacetic acid and interferon injections. Recent studies show that infrared coagulation is a safe procedure performed under local anesthesia on patients with discrete high-grade squamous lesions. The device uses a beam of far-infrared light.

The anal Pap smear is a simple test that is performed by your doctor in his office. It involves swabbing the anus with a Dacron swab, which looks like a long Q-Tip. The swab is then smeared on slides and sent to the pathologist. This test is so important because there are many different types of HPV. The most common are types 6, 11, 16, and 18. Certain subtypes, specifically 16 and 18, are considered precancerous. As a patient, you should report any cauliflowerlike lesions that develop on your skin because HPV can show up on your penis, anus, and even your tongue.

In 2006, Merck & Co delivered the first vaccine for HPV called Gardasil. It is a quadrivalent vaccine, which means it works on HPV subtypes 6, 11, 16, and 18, and it is given in three separate injections over six months. Currently, the vaccine is indicated only for women, but the majority of gay health-care providers are urging their gay male patients to consider this vaccine, especially those men who are HIV positive or have a history of HPV. At this time the vaccine is not covered by insurance and would have to be paid for out of pocket. Presently, Merck

Dr. Frank's Tips on Watching for HPV

1. Talk to your doctor about HPV, the Pap smear, and the vaccine.
2. Any bumps or lesions on your penis, scrotum, or anus should be reported to your doctor.
3. Get a digital rectal exam and Pap smear.
4. Use condoms—they reduce the risk of transmitting HPV.
5. Stop smoking. It has been found that smoking is related to HPV's progression to cancer.

is studying this vaccine in 4,000 young men, including those who engage in sex with other men, and the National Institutes of Health (NIH) is evaluating the response to Merck's vaccine in preteen HIV-positive boys and girls.

PROSTATE SCREENING

Prostate cancer is one of the most common cancers and is the second leading cause of cancer deaths among men in the United States. When detected early, prostate cancer can be treated effectively and cured. In addition to the rectal exam, which checks the size, shape, and consistency of the prostate, the Prostate Specific Antigen, or PSA, aids in the diagnosis for the possibility of cancer. The PSA is a blood test that measures the amount of enzyme that is produced by the prostate (normal is 0–4ng/mL). Increased PSAs can be associated with inflammation of the prostate, called *prostatitis*, which is commonly caused by infection and can also be linked to prostate cancer. Manipulation of the prostate can yield increased PSAs, and so it is not recommended, especially just after a digital rectal exam or after recipient anal sex. Gay men over age forty should be screened annually for prostate disease with a digital rectal exam and a PSA.

The actual cause of prostate cancer is unknown, but we do know that it is more common in African-American men and men with a family history of the disease. The male sex hormone testosterone also contributes to its growth. The American Cancer Society estimates that over 200,000 men in the United States will be diagnosed with prostate cancer this year and more than 30,000 will die of the disease. Overall, about one in six men will be diagnosed with prostate cancer, but only one of thirty-four will die of it. About 80 percent of men who reach age eighty have prostate cancer, but that doesn't mean we are all going to die from prostate cancer. This is a slow-growing cancer; nearly 100 percent of men with prostate cancer survive at least five years after their diagnosis, 93 percent survive at least ten years, and 67 percent survive longer than fifteen years.

SEXUALLY TRANSMITTED DISEASES SCREENING

Venereal is taken from the word *Venus*, the goddess of love in Roman mythology. *Venereal disease* (VD) has been replaced by the more contemporary term *sexually transmitted diseases* (STD), which describes infections that are passed on during sexual intercourse, whether it is anal, oral, or vaginal. Due to the higher rates of anonymous sex and sex associated with Internet chat room, gay men have a higher risk of developing STDs. Common STDs include gonorrhea, chlamydia, syphilis, herpes, pubic lice (crabs), scabies, hepatitis A, B, C, parasites, and the human papillomavirus (HPV). To reduce your chances of infection, follow these suggestions:

> *Use condoms correctly every time you have sex.*
> *Urinate after ejaculation.*
> *Limit the number of sex partners.*
> *If you think you are infected, avoid sexual contact and see a doctor.*

HIV SCREENING

HIV, or the human immunodeficiency virus, attacks the immune system, your body's defense mechanism against infection. One of the most important components of the immune system is CD4 cells, or T-cells. HIV attacks T-cells and is passed from one person to the next by contact with blood or other bodily fluids, like semen. The usual mode for gay men is unsafe anal intercourse. Studies suggest that you are infected not at the immediate time of exposure to HIV but after a window up to seventy-two hours. Usually, symptoms develop after four to six weeks and include fever, headache, tiredness, and enlarged lymph nodes, or what we call a mononucleosis-type syndrome. "Mono" is the kissing disease some of you might have had as a teenager. HIV antibodies, however, can take from three to even twelve months to develop in a person. This mechanism of converting to HIV-positive is called seroconversion. Once you have seroconverted, you can detect HIV antibodies in the blood, but you may not have any symptoms. If left untreated, HIV is a fatal disease. Currently, there is no cure for HIV, but the development of many treatments over the past two decades has made it largely a chronic, manageable disease.

Back in 1981, the CDC reported five gay men who were being treated for *Pneumocystis carinii* pneumonia, which later was determined to be AIDS-related; however, it is believed that HIV was detected as early as 1959. In 1982, the term *AIDS*, or acquired immune deficiency syndrome, was coined. The NIH defines AIDS as an advanced stage of HIV usually marked by a T-cell count less than 200 cells per milliliter of blood. This allows "opportunistic" infections to develop, which are severe and sometimes fatal, because the body can no longer fight them. It was not until 1987 that the first drug, AZT (retrovir), was approved for the treatment of HIV. Later, with the development of the protease inhibitors, the mortality rate from HIV was greatly diminished. HAART, or highly active antiretroviral treatment, was established as the standard of care, and the term *cocktail* was used to describe the increasing number of multidrug regimens available to treat HIV.

Men who have sex with men (MSM) are at an increased risk of developing HIV. From 2002 to 2006, the CDC reported a growing trend of 10 percent in the number of new cases of HIV. This led to their recommendation that HIV testing be made available to all patients thirteen years and older if they are sexually active. More alarming is the fact that new diagnoses have doubled among New York City MSM ages thirteen to nineteen. Despite the decline in older men, there exists a sense of complacency concerning HIV. The disease is manage-

IN THE SAME WEEK that the CDC made their announcement, I did a phone interview with CBS radio to give my opinion. Before we went on air, the producer briefed me that there had been a harsh outcry against the CDC's recommendation and that there were many people against it. This seemed ridiculous to me. Why would you not want to know if you were HIV positive? This is a question that has come up time and again. I have attended lectures and dinner parties where I heard gay men admit to me that they would not want to know if they were HIV positive. Therefore, it was not a complete shock when the CBS reporter told me that the heterosexual population had their own reservations as well.

able but to relegate it as another chronic condition like diabetes could be dangerous. The fact is there is a lack of familiarity among younger gay men concerning the AIDS epidemic. Categorizing HIV as a chronic disease makes many gay men feel that it is less of a threat. There are even some who see HIV as "no big deal" and make the assumption that it is an inevitable part of life. Despite the clear benefits of a "one-pill-once-a-day regimen," HIV is still considered incurable and some men

1959	Scientists isolate what is believed to be the earliest known case of AIDS
1978	Gay men in the U.S. begin showing signs of what will later be called AIDS
1981	The Centers for Disease Control reports that five homosexual men were treated for *Pneumocystis carinii* pneumonia which was later determined to be AIDS related
1982	The term AIDS is coined The Gay Men's Health Crisis, GMHC, is established in New York City
1985	The FDA approves the first HIV-antibody test President Ronald Reagan mentions AIDS for the first time in a public speech
1986	Actor Rock Hudson dies from AIDS
1987	AZT becomes the first drug approved for the treatment of HIV. ACT UP (AIDS Coalition to Unleash Power) is founded in New York City
1990	Ryan White dies at age eighteen from AIDS President Reagan apologizes for his neglect of the AIDS crisis during his presidency Fashion designer Halston dies from AIDS
1991	Basketball player Magic Johnson announces that he has HIV
1992	Actor Robert Reed from TV's *The Brady Bunch* dies from AIDS
1995	Olympic diver Greg Louganis reveals that he has AIDS
1996	The number of deaths from AIDS in the U.S. is nearly 35,000 *Time* magazine announces researcher David Ho as Man of the Year
1997	AIDS-related deaths decline in the U.S. by more than 40 percent due largely to HAART (highly active anti-retroviral therapy)
2002	HIV is the leading cause of death worldwide, among those aged 15–59 The FDA approves the Oraquick, the first rapid HIV test
2006	There are over 1 million cases of HIV in the U.S., and one out of four individuals who are HIV+are not diagnosed The CDC announces its recommendation that all individuals who are sexually active should be screened for HIV
2007	New York State Board of Health publishes statistics indicating that HIV rates among MSM under age thirty have increased 33 percent Merck halts HIV vaccine trial after the study failed to show it reduced the risk of infection; the international trial was the latest in a long line of disappointments in HIV vaccines

The HIV/AIDS Timeline in Brief

do not respond to drug therapy. The main questions concerning HIV is: How would you view having any other chronic disease? Would you want to be diabetic if you had the choice? Certainly no one should want to be infected especially when it can be prevented. As for those who are positive, of course the simplicity and potency of the newer regimens has altered the course of HIV. Now those who are positive can expect to live out their full life expectancy; yet diminishing this disease as "no big deal" could be further misconstrued by a generation of younger gay men.

As of 2007, there were over one million people in the United States infected with HIV, and of those about 25 percent don't know they have it. Even more frightening is the fact that nearly 25 percent of people with HIV are, at the time of diagnosis, already in an advanced state of AIDS. Back in the 1980s, a diagnosis of HIV was considered a death sentence. Fortunately, that is not the case anymore. There are many treatment options available now, with fewer pills and better tolerability. It is estimated that if someone is diagnosed with HIV, they can live out their full life as long as they maintain their health. The key is education with an emphasis on prevention, but more important is the knowledge you've been infected.

The current recommendation for HIV screening is annually; however, for sexually active MSMs, I recommend every three to six months.

IMMUNIZATIONS AND VACCINES

The word *vaccine* calls to mind the great smallpox epidemic that affected Great Britain. This was a virus transmitted through cattle called cow pox that was contracted by humans when milking their cows. In 1796, Edward Jenner developed the vaccine for smallpox, essentially wiping it out. The practice of vaccination has extended over the whole civilized world, and its value in preventing disease is a testament to the men that discovered them.

FIVE VACCINES THAT EVERY GAY MAN SHOULD KNOW ABOUT

Tetanus, diptheria (Td) and tetanus, diptheria, and acellular pertussis (Tdap) vaccination

1. Tetanus vaccine

Tetanus is an often-fatal disease caused by the bacteria *Clostridium tetani*. Contracted through injuries such as lacerations, punctures, and splinters, tetanus is characterized by muscular rigidity rapidly spreading throughout the body, producing pain and stiffness, especially in the neck and jaw—hence the alternative name lockjaw. The impact on the facial muscles produces a particular characteristic feature called *risus sardonicus*, or "sardonic grin," in which the angles of the mouth are drawn down, exposing taught clenched teeth. The vaccine for tetanus is co-administered with the diphtheria toxoid called Td, which should be offered to all adults. Administration of a booster dose to all adults who have completed a primary series can be given after ten years. A new one-time single dose of Tdap instead of Td is recommended for those between the ages of nineteen and sixty-four in order to provide protection against the spread of pertussis.

2. Hepatitis A and B vaccine

Both hepatitis A and B are viruses that can be avoided through vaccination. By the very nature of their sexual practices, gay men are more predisposed to these diseases, and it is strongly recommend that they all get vaccinated, especially those who are HIV-positive. Prior to taking the vaccination, your doctor should check your blood for the antibodies because you could already have been exposed to hepatitis A or B and not know it. If you have not been exposed, and that is proven by a blood test, then your doctor can administer the series. Hepatitis B is given in three separate injections over six months. Hepatitis A is given twice over six months. The combined hepatitis A and B, or the TWINRX, is given three times over six months. Once you have completed the series, immunity is assessed by checking for the anitibodies in your blood. Upon development of the antibodies, you will have immunity against hepatitis for up to seven to ten years. The vaccine has been available in the United States since 1995.

3. Pneumovax

This is a preventative vaccine against pneumococcal pneumonia caused by the bacteria streptococcus pneumonia. The indication is for individuals, aged sixty-five and older, or anyone with chronic medical conditions, such as diabetes, liver disease, kidney failure, and especially HIV. A booster shot after five years can be given.

4. Flu vaccine

Every fall there is a huge campaign for the flu vaccine. The flu can be debilitating and even deadly for some who contract it. A few years ago there was even a shortage of the flu vaccine. This had everyone in a panic. The CDC reports that each year the flu will affect 5 to 20 percent of the population and more than 200,000 people will be hospitalized from complications of it. In fact, about 35,000 people will die from the flu each year. An allergy to eggs is the only excuse to avoid the flu vaccine because current manufacturers use an egg extract as the basis for the vaccine.

5. Gardasil

The vaccine for the human papillomavirus (HPV) types 6, 11, 16, and 18. Currently this vaccine is not indicated in men. Gardasil helps prevent disease and does not treat HPV. It works best when given before you have had any contact with HPV.

THE TUBERCULIN SKIN TEST OR PURIFIED PROTEIN DERIVATIVE (PPD)

The PPD is not a vaccine, but a screening test to detect exposure to tuberculosis. Tuberculosis is a disease caused by the bacteria *Mycobacterium tuberculosis*. Formerly known as "consumption"—for all you opera fans—this bacterial infection commonly affects the lungs but can also spread to other parts of the body (extrapulmonary TB). TB in the lungs is easily spread to other people through simple coughing. In Puccini's opera, *La Bohème,* Mimi contracts tuberculosis and dies at the end. Today, there is treatment for this disease, but it involves a multidrug protocol that can average from six to nine months.

The PPD is a useful screening tool to detect exposure to TB because everyone exposed to tuberculosis does not necessarily develop the disease. Any health-care provider can administer a PPD, which involves injecting a small amount of inactive TB into your skin. After 48 hours, the area injected is checked to detect a skin reaction. If the area is red or raised, then this is a positive PPD. Only a health-care provider can determine this because the area of swelling must be measured. All positive PPDs should be followed up with a chest X-ray. If the X-ray shows no evidence of lung tuberculosis, then your health-care provider should discuss taking the antibiotic called isoniazide as a prophylaxis against developing tuberculosis in the future. Annual PPDs are recommended for all patients, especially those who are HIV positive, but if you know you are PPD positive, then make sure to tell your health-care provider. This test should not be repeated, for fear of a stronger reaction to the PPD.

DEPRESSION AND ANXIETY

Depression affects six million men in the United States. Although it has been noted that men are less likely to be affected by depression than women, studies suggest that men are less inclined to complain about it to their doctors. Several large surveys suggest a higher prevalence of psychiatric disorders among gay men. Conversely, the suicide rates in men are four times higher than in women; however, women attempt it more often.

There is a debate concerning whether gay men on the whole suffer from depression more than their heterosexual counterparts. The fact is that gay teenagers are more likely to suffer from depression due to the stress of "coming out," while others struggle with discovering their sexuality, knowing that they are "different" from their peers. Adolescent gay men even have higher rates of suicide. Likewise, many adult gay men struggle with the complex issue of "coming out" and the apprehension over being a societal anomaly. In the HIV community, mental illness is a frequent issue, most often due to the debilitating nature of the disease, but also due to the battle in coming to grips with the diagnosis. Reports suggest that the rates of major depression, bipolar disorder, and obsessive compulsive behavior in HIV-positive patients can be as high as 54 percent. Other studies have shown that untreated depression can even increase the progression to AIDS in this population.

A recent report by the *American Journal of Psychiatry* found that there were indeed higher rates of depression in gay men than in the general population. As a result, gay men are more likely to engage in high-risk sexual behavior and to abuse alcohol and drugs with more frequency. Inadequate social support, internalized homophobia, shame over not meeting cultural standards, and cultural insensitivity were cited as some of the many reasons that gay men fall prey to depression.

The World Health Organization categorizes depression into typical, mild, moderate, or severe episodes. Patients with depression may suffer from low energy, decreased activity, and depressed mood. Often there is a diminished capacity for enjoyment and interests. Concentration is reduced, and there can be marked lethargy even in performing minimal tasks. Depressed men complain about disturbed sleep patterns in which they either sleep too much or suffer from insomnia. Appetite is usually affected in much the same way, with patients complaining that they eat too much or too little. Usually the depressed male expresses feelings of low self-worth, lack of self-esteem, and diminished self-confidence. Men with prolonged depression describe a sense of utter worthlessness and associated guilt. Moods can vary from one day to the next and are often accompanied by "somatic" complaints, such as body aches and pains. One of the most striking complaints for gay men is a loss of sexual interest and pronounced erectile dysfunction.

The three major depressive disorders include:

1. Major depression, which is characterized by symptoms that interfere with the ability to work, sleep, or eat, and persist for at least two weeks. These episodes may occur only once but usually crop up several times in a lifetime. Major depressive episodes without symptoms of mania have also been referred to as unipolar depression. The diagnosis of major depression excludes cases where the symptoms are a result of normal bereavement as in loss of a loved one, except when it persists for a period of over one year.

2. Dysthymia is characterized by a less severe form of depression. Symptoms are more chronic, lasting for at least two years with brief periods of improvement but for no more then two months. Patients are usually not disabled by their symptoms. In fact they usually carry on their normal daily functions; however, they are unable to perform to the best of their ability and are usually dissatisfied with their performance.

3. Bipolar disorder, also called manic-depressive illness, is characterized by episodes of mania followed by severe depression. Mania is described as an extreme change in mood that is often dramatic and energetic. During the manic phase the patient may appear overactive and

talkative. Manic episodes affect a patient's rational thinking and judgment. Commonly, they may go on expensive shopping sprees and proclaim to have grand schemes. Socially their behavior is inappropriate and can be embarrassing. Usually the manic person dresses wildly with vibrant colors. Untreated, the manic episode can worsen into a psychotic state. The transition from depression into mania can be rapid or gradual, but there is a marked change in mood. In the depressed phase, symptoms are consistent with major depression.

Signs and symptoms to look for that might lead you to believe that you or someone you know is depressed include:

1. Constant fatigue
2. Insomnia or sleeping throughout the day
3. Disinterest in normal activities
4. Increased use of recreational drugs or alcohol
5. Sad or irritable mood
6. Tearfulness and feelings of despair
7. Change in appetite with either weight loss or weight gain

Despite the different categories of depression, anxiety may often co-exist. The National Comorbidity Survey (U.S.) reports that 58 percent of those with major depression also suffer from episodes of anxiety. It is also evident that even mild symptoms of anxiety can have a major impact on the course of a depressed individual.

The National Institutes of Mental Health (NIMH)

define generalized anxiety disorder (GAD) as chronic anxiety, exaggerated worry, and prolonged tension, even when there is little or nothing to provoke it. People with GAD are often preoccupied with their health, money, and family issues. Usually they find that even the least troublesome task can be thoroughly anxiety producing.

GAD is excessive worry that persists for at least six months. Most patients are even able to rationalize that their worry is unwarranted; however, they are still unable to find comfort or relax, even after discussing their fears openly. Most patients with GAD have an incredibly difficult time concentrating and suffer from erratic sleep patterns.

One patient, David, had a longstanding history of bi-polar disorder and such severe anxiety that he suffered from an inability to swallow. This issue complicated his treatment because he had trouble taking medication. After a battery of tests that included an upper endoscopy, he was diagnosed with a narrowing of the esophagus. Despite multiple attempts at dilating the stricture, David still had a poor capacity to swallow and needed to crush all his medications.

Other common symptoms associated with anxiety include headaches, nausea, heart palpitations, and short-ness of breath. In mild cases of GAD, most patients can function socially and maintain a job. In more severe cases, patients instinctively avoid situations that are considered anxiety provoking; in some instances, this can interfere with basic daily activities. Social phobias and post-traumatic stress disorder are other forms of anxiety.

In order to make the diagnosis of GAD, symptoms must persist for longer than six months and have to include at least three of the following:

> *fatigue*
> *irritability*
> *insomnia or excessive sleep*
> *muscle tension*
> *restlessness*
> *difficulty focusing*

Like depression, GAD is treated with behavioral therapy and medication. For the most part, depression and anxiety are said to be 40 to 70 percent inheritable, according to the NIMH.

In addition to family history, gay men endure issues with low self-esteem and shame. Often the complex development of a gay man's personality and learning how to cope with environmental stress are also major contributing factors toward mental illness. Traumatic experiences especially during childhood involving bereavement, neglect, or abuse can increase the likelihood of depression. Even certain chronic medical conditions like HIV, hepatitis, and hypothyroidism can contribute to depression. Particularly in some gay men, struggles with anabolic steroids, alcohol, benzodiazepines, and recreational drugs can complicate a patient's battle with psychiatric problems.

With the current state of health care, primary-care providers are faced with the unwanted task of having to treat many common psychiatric illnesses like depression and anxiety. Many doctors increasingly have to attend to these conditions as the "gatekeeper" to all illnesses. Most clinicians agree that screening for depression and anxiety in the gay community is warranted.

Essentially, there are chemical changes or imbalances that affect how information is transmitted in the brain. These neurotransmitters affect mood. Decreased levels of certain ones, specifically serotonin and norepinephrine, can result in depression and anxiety. Medications that target these neurotransmitters are called selective serotonin re-uptake inhibitors, or SSRIs. This class of drugs includes such popular brands as Prozac (fluoxetine), Zoloft (sertraline), Paxil (paroxetine), and Lexapro (escitalopram oxalate). SSRIs work well to alleviate symptoms of depression and GAD but also help restore the brain's chemical imbalances. Recent advances in psychopharmacology have produced another class of antidepressants that target both serotonin and norepinephrine, called serotonin norepinephrine re-uptake inhibitors (SNRIs). One example is Cymbalta (duloxetine HCL), which in addition to its antidepressant affects also treats such somatic complaints as bodily pain. Still another commonly used antidepressant medication, Wellbutrin (buproprion), works as a norepinephrine/dopamine re-uptake inhibitor. With all these different classes of drugs, making the appropriate choice can be a difficult decision, especially when you have to consider all the different side effects.

As a whole, the SSRIs are associated with sexual side effects, sleep disturbances, as well as weight gain. This can be alarming for some patients; however, it is my experience that they are well tolerated. Before you begin any drug regimen your doctor should discuss not only the potential side effects but also how the medication works and any drug interactions. Most antidepressants take effect after one or two weeks but require two to four weeks for full effect.

Another class of drugs called benzodiazepines, known for their sedating effect, were widely overused in the 1960s and 1970s to alleviate stress but were found to be highly addictive. Many patients to this day request these medications, which include Valium, Xanax, Ativan, and Klonopin because of their immediate onset of action. Unfortunately, they only provide temporary relief of symptoms and tolerance can soon develop. Benzodiazepines are not recommended for long-term treatment of anxiety or depression. They may be necessary for an acute breakthrough of anxiety, but caution needs to be exercised because of the addiction potential.

For the most part, patients usually require antidepressants to aid them through difficult periods in their lives, like the death of a loved one, the loss of a job, or a break-up. In these cases, antidepressants are prescribed for a specific period of time, usually six months to a year. In many cases, especially in complicated circumstances, therapy is also called for.

Traditional psychotherapy can be an essential outlet for most patients experiencing depression or anxiety. It allows some people the ability to express their underlying fears and concerns, while for others it affords the chance to explore more deeply rooted issues. In addition to traditional one-on-one therapy, there is also group therapy. This is a form of psychotherapy in which one or several therapists treat a small group of patients. Sometimes this is essential because of the cost-effectiveness compared to one-on-one counseling. In a group, the members organize around related issues and try to resolve them as a system. This gives the members the opportunity to explore personal issues within a social context.

Feelings of prolonged depression and anxiety should be brought to your health-care provider's attention. There are many treatment options available, and no one should have to suffer.

Other psychosocial concerns that affect gay men include addiction, especially to alcohol, tobacco, and drugs. Questions regarding eating disorders, especially bulimia and anorexia, should be addressed as well during the initial assessment. Finally, other complex issues that come up time and again for gay men include concerns with sexual compulsivity, domestic violence, and hate crimes.

SMOKING, ALCOHOL, AND RECREATIONAL DRUGS

Tobacco use has been a long-standing health care problem with its association to lung cancer, heart disease, and strokes. An estimated 25.5 million men and 21.5 million women in the U.S. smoke, as reported by the American Heart and Lung Association. In some recent studies, it has been shown that tobacco use is higher among gay men, reaching nearly 50 percent in several studies. Counseling patients about tobacco abuse is frustrating because, despite all the evidence that we have, indicating its addictiveness and carcinogenicity, we still smoke.

So why do we smoke?

Most people claim they smoke to alleviate stress. Others model their behavior after their parents or people they admire. Many smoke because of peer pressure or wanting to look cool like movie stars and musicians. How hot was Brad Pitt in *Fight Club*, all cut up and smoldering, or the cast of *Chicago*, lighting up their cigarettes, singing and dancing in that dark nightclub? The allure of smoking is so intense and sexual that it was destined to be part of our culture. Smoking gives the illusion of self-confidence and maturity—how could any gay man resist?

There are many different methods to quit smoking. Success requires a willingness to quit. The National Cancer Institute states that even a brief counseling session with a health-care provider will more than likely result

WHEN I ASK patients about their smoking, I document their "pack-year history." This is the number of packs of cigarettes smoked per day times the number of smoking years. It is estimated that if you have less than a ten-pack-year history then the chance of your lungs returning to their normal functional capacity is greater than if you smoked more. I tell all of my patients that it usually takes a full year to begin to feel the benefits from not smoking. This includes a decrease in coughing, improved taste, and better lung function. I know this for a fact, because even I smoked at one time.

in a cessation of smoking. Most clinicians agree that the best way to quit is "cold turkey," as opposed to weaning yourself off slowly. Before you quit, select a stop date. This will give you ample time to prepare. Some patients utilize nicotine-replacement therapy with the patch or gum. Remember that if you do relapse, remove the patch so as to avoid being exposed to high levels of nicotine.

There are various forms of drug therapy available to facilitate an end to smoking. Zyban (bupropion) has been studied extensively and is FDA-approved as a treatment to help smokers quit. (Incidentally, this is the same

Dr. Frank's 10 Tips on How to Quit Smoking

1. Set a date to quit and stop smoking completely. Don't even take a puff.
2. Get rid of all cigarettes, even your secret stash.
3. Don't let people smoke around you. It's too tempting.
4. Get support from your friends and family.
5. Consider group counseling.
6. Learn stress-reduction techniques, like exercising or walking, to avoid the urge.
7. Drink lots of water.
8. Talk to your doctor about the different types of medications that are now available.
9. Consider getting counseling by telephone at 800-QUIT-NOW.
10. Be prepared for relapses, and if you do fall off the wagon, get right back on it.

medication that is used to treat depression under the brand-name Wellbutrin.) Smokers take bupropion orally for one to two weeks while they smoke and then continue the medication after they have reached their quit date. Bupropion is not indicated in patients who suffer from seizure disorder. The most common side effects include insomnia; however there are fewer reported cases of weight gain and sexual side effects than with other antidepressants. Also the antidepressant action of bupropion helps smokers during the crucial period after they have stopped smoking.

In May 2006, the FDA approved Chantix (varenicline tartrate), another oral medication that is designed to help smokers quit. Chantix acts at sites in the brain that are affected by nicotine. This will ease the withdrawal symptoms and blunt the response of nicotine if you resume smoking. As with bupropion, varenicline is a pill that is taken orally each day for one to two weeks. You continue to smoke until you reach your stop date and then continue varenicline for at least twelve weeks. Common side effects include nausea, gas, and vomiting. Both bupropion and varenicline usually generate good results. If you wish to stop smoking, consult your doctor about these options.

According to the CDC, an estimated 45 million adults smoke in the United States and more than 8 million of them have at least one serious illness caused by smoking. Tobacco is the single most preventable cause of death in the United States and is responsible for a growing list of cancers.

Smoking has also been linked to erectile dysfunction in numerous clinical studies. The most common causes of the organic component in erectile dysfunction, or impotence, are vascular abnormalities associated with atherosclerosis and diabetes mellitus. Atherosclerosis causes 40 percent of cases of erectile dysfunction, and in cases of diabetes mellitus the prevalence of erectile dysfunction is 50 percent. Smoking is significantly associated with the development of both atherosclerosis and diabetes mellitus.

Researchers at Wake Forest University in Winston-Salem, North Carolina, concluded that male smokers who suffer from long-standing hypertension are twenty-six times more likely to be impotent than those individuals who do not smoke. Aside from impotence, smoking has also been linked to the following negative effects concerning male sexual health:

> *Reduced volume of ejaculation*
> *Lowered sperm count*
> *Abnormal sperm shape*
> *Impaired sperm motility*

In addition to smoking, there is always a point in a person's life when he feels compelled to liberate himself from his adolescent self by succumbing to the temptations that we have all been warned against as children. Alcohol, like smoking, has an enticing appeal, yet its consequences are just as devastating for some people.

While some can control their ability to drink socially, others cannot. The debilitating effects alcohol can have on the human body, whether your liver or your judgment, are well known. Thousands die each year at the hands of a drunk driver. Nearly 17.6 million adult Americans currently abuse alcohol, according to the National Institute of Alcohol Abuse and Alcoholism. Several million more engage in risky drinking that could lead to alcohol problems. These patterns include binge drinking and heavy drinking on a regular basis. Not surprisingly, alcohol use and dependence is common among gay men.

Textbook factors that contribute to alcohol dependence include feelings of internalized homophobia, which can lead to psychological stress. Often, gay men experience their first sexual encounter under the influence of alcohol. This can develop into a vicious cycle. In order to overcome their inhibitions about their sexuality, some men drink and then blame their behavior on the alcohol. Acceptance is the key to recovery in gay men. Risk factors for alcohol dependence include men who have a family history of alcohol abuse or those who were exposed to alcohol growing up. Drinking at an early age has been associated with developing problems with alcohol in the future.

Concerning alcohol consumption, you should expect to answer questions regarding exactly how much you drink. Many gay men consider themselves social drinkers, which is an evasive a response when a doctor asks a patient about drinking. Expect to hear from your doctor: "How often do you socialize?" It is also important to understand what you consider a "drink." Is it a glass of wine a night, a shot of bourbon, or a six-pack of beer? Everyone's perception is different. Ask yourself, "How often do I drink?" You will be surprised. Gay men underestimate three things in life: how much they drink, how much they smoke, and how much they have sex. Indications that you, or someone you know, has a drinking problem include:

1. Problems at work or missing work
2. Numerous injuries attributed to falling or being accident-prone
3. Drinking and driving
4. Blacking out or unexplained loss of consciousness
5. Medical problems like peptic ulcer disease

Many people consider themselves "social drinkers" because they do not drink every day; however, drinking excessively on the weekends can also qualify as abuse. That is why it is so important to realize that you do not need to drink every day to have a problem. Also, some

SOMETIMES it is very difficult to identify patients who have a problem with alcohol. I took care of an elderly gay couple for years, and never knew that one was alcohol dependent. When the older of the two suffered a heart attack, he pleaded with me that if anything should happen to him, then I would look after his partner. Then he confided in me that his lover went to bed drunk every night. I had been doctor to them both for years and never suspected a thing. After his recovery, I confronted his partner who swore he only drank one or two martinis a night. Even if this was true, the reality of stumbling to bed each night was a sure sign that his drinking was out of control. Alcohol dependence does not necessitate drinking large quantities of alcohol every day, and therefore it may be hard for someone to recognize their own battle with the bottle.

people can cease all alcohol consumption for days, weeks, or even months before they start drinking again. To consistently maintain control of your alcohol intake, once you have identified it as a problem, takes professional help and social support.

Naltrexone, an opioid receptor antagonist, is used primarily in the management of alcohol dependence. In 2006, the FDA-approved naltrexone extended-release injection under the brand-name Vivitrol, which is administered monthly by a health-care professional for the treatment of alcohol dependence. Vivitrol does not eliminate or diminish alcohol withdrawal symptoms but acts to reduce the craving for alcohol. The product is indicated for use with psychosocial support in patients who are able to abstain from drinking in an outpatient setting and are not actively drinking on initiation of therapy.

Alcoholics Anonymous is a very helpful resource in the treatment of gay alcohol dependence. A.A. meetings offer support as well as counseling, and they are not as religious as some people fear. Most cities even have gay, or gay-friendly, A.A. meetings, which is extremely helpful for gay clients who might not identify with heterosexuals. A.A. even has pamphlets for the gay alcohol dependent.

In addition to A.A., gay men with alcohol and drug issues should be referred for psychotherapy or counseling in order to get evaluated for depression and internalized homophobia. It is imperative that their support system be adequate to ensure their recovery. Recovering from alcohol and drugs often involves facing the same problems as anyone else who has gone through the process of recovery. Patients must learn to give up old friends and stay away from bars and other places that might instigate a relapse. Individuals undergoing recovery must learn to be comfortable without drugs and alcohol and accept a life without them. One of the most important aspects for gay men is learning to cope with the people around you who continue to use drugs and alcohol. Sometimes there is no escaping the temptation. Relapse is extremely common. Those people who do relapse should not be deterred and should get right back up and try again.

As for recreational drugs, gay men use them at higher rates than the general population, and a number of substances are favored by gay men: amyl nitrite (poppers), marijuana, ecstasy, crystal, special K, cocaine, and GHB (G).

Recreational drugs are a form of escapism. Their history has been documented for years and whether you are using prescription drugs or street drugs, the belief that you are taking something to "let go" or to "have a good time" is equivalent.

Substance abuse is a major crisis among gay men. The crystal methamphetamine epidemic has certainly become its own separate dilemma when gay men are contracting HIV in record numbers because of their crystal use. But what about all of those gay men who are not addicts? In our community there exists a form of drug dependence called "functional addiction." Simply put, they are individuals who are able to live, work, and pay bills while using recreational drugs on a routine or even daily basis. This issue almost surpasses those who are clearly physically and emotionally dependant because there is a certain underlying denial with functional addicts.

For gay men, the establishment of drug use is as much a part of their psychosocial assessment as their smoking and alcohol intake. Most men admit to occasional drug use on "party weekends." So then, the question becomes how many "party weekends" are there in a year? If you log onto www.CircuitNoize.com, you can probably find a party somewhere in the world on any given day. The use

I ASK ALL MY PATIENTS if they use recreational or "party" drugs. Once I had a patient who worked for a leading fashion designer as director of marketing. He was bright, intelligent, and very successful. Unfortunately, he was also quite paranoid. He was worried that his phone conversations were being tapped and he was convinced that his employers were about to fire him. I inquired how he knew this, and he reiterated that he "just knew." Later I asked him if he took recreational drugs and he told me that he didn't "party" anymore but that he snorted crystal once a day before going to work. He was convinced that this one "bump" gave him self-confidence and boosted his morale. Needless to say, he was not happy when I tried to argue that this one "bump" was also making him paranoid and delusional.

of recreational drugs at circuit parties is a fact. The worrisome issue is how much and to what extent.

It is important to ask yourself these questions:

> *Why do I use recreational drugs?*
> *How often do I party?*

> *Have I ever missed work because of excessive partying?*

Mothers may have warned you that what makes you feel good can't be good for you, though they may have been innocently referring to potato chips or candy, not ecstasy or "blow." Maybe the idea of being tempted by forbidden fruit is something we will all have to struggle with at one time or another, but know this: Too many gay men lose their lives to GHB. In 1999, there were nearly 3,000 medical emergencies related to GHB, and the Drug Enforcement Agency reported sixty GHB-related deaths in 2000.

Likewise, too many young men have suffered heart attacks from cocaine use. The American Heart Association reported that regular cocaine use is associated with an increased likelihood of heart attacks in younger men. Independent risk factors for heart attacks include older age, race, male sex, and hereditary factors. Compounded by cocaine use, the risk of a heart attack in the first hour after usage is twenty-four-times greater than normal, as reported by the University of Michigan Health System in 2003, and cocaine users have a sevenfold lifetime risk of a heart attack.

If you use recreational drugs, please be honest with your doctor, and if you think you have a problem, then seek counseling, whether through your doctor or on-line. There are many resources listed in the back of this book.

In the United States, gay men constitute the highest population infected with HIV. Alcohol and recreational drugs have been shown to be associated with a higher risk for unsafe sex. Alcohol, smoking, and recreational drug use is conducive to poor compliance with prescribed medication and promotes premature progression of other illnesses like diabetes, hypertension, and HIV. Treatment, especially for alcohol and substance abuse, needs to focus not only on the disorder, but also on acceptance of one's homosexuality.

NUTRITIONAL ASSESSMENT

Every physical exam should include a nutritional assessment. Currently, over 58 million Americans are clinically obese. A sedentary lifestyle and a poor diet contribute to obesity. I often wish I had a dollar for every time I heard someone tell me that the reason they are fat is because they have a thyroid or "glandular" problem. For the majority of people this is a falsity. Eating poorly and not exercising makes you fat. True, there is some validity that obesity has a genetic component, but there are things you can do to achieve a healthier body.

A nutritional assessment consists of the patient's height, weight, and blood chemistries. For most people, stepping on a scale is torture. However, for those who struggle with weight, it is important to know that monitoring trends is more valuable than any one particular measure.

Ideal body weight for a man is estimated as 106 pounds for the first five feet and then six pounds for every inch over that. For example, a 5-foot, 7-inch man should weigh approximately 148 pounds. However, there is a range of roughly 20 percent above and below this number, depending on bone structure and muscularity, that would still be considered normal. A very muscular male will weigh more because muscles carry more mass then fat. In order to assess if an individual is obese or underweight, it is better to use the body mass index, or BMI, which measures weight in kilograms divided by height in meters squared: BMI=kg/m2. These measurements may be reserved for extreme cases, especially HIV-positive men who also need input from a nutritionist. In HIV-positive patients BMIs have become a very useful tool because in advanced cases, patients lose lean muscle mass, and as a result standard weights are not completely accurate to assess for wasting.

Furthermore, bioelectrical impedance analysis (BIA) is another simple technique used to determine body composition. Four electrodes are attached to the patient's wrist and ankle on the same side of the body while a painless alternating current is passed through him. From the BIA, it is possible to estimate body cell mass, fat-free mass, and other useful parameters.

In assessing nutritional status, a conversation about a patient's diet and exercise regimen should be established. A major concern for most men over forty is getting their bodies back into shape. Relevant lifestyle modifications can be discussed, but it is essential that in order to achieve a better body that you understand the basics.

No discussion about your physical well-being can begin without asking a patient what it is about their body they are not happy with. For the majority it means either losing weight or gaining muscle mass. In order to do this, you need to establish realistic goals. Losing ten pounds in one week is neither realistic nor healthy. Most become frustrated at the thought of changing their bodies. Many people are scarred by memories of extreme diets and torturous exercise plans. The important thing to remember before you begin any program is that this is not supposed to be a painful journey. Changing your body requires learning healthier habits. Lifestyle modification has to be your mantra. You are embarking on a new way of life, not a crash course in body shaping.

The best way to reshape and sculpt your body is through weight training. Aerobic exercise will help you lose weight, but weight training is what promotes fat loss. Joining a gym is imperative before you begin any workout program. You may prefer working out in public as opposed to your home because a gym is highly motivating. Being around other people will push you to work out harder. If you have sufficient funds, it is wise to obtain a personal trainer. Trainers will be able to show you the basics of working out. Learning good habits early will help you to avoid injuries in the future. Also trainers are highly motivating and get you to work out harder than if you were by yourself. Working out with a partner is a good alternative if you can't afford a trainer. Remember to start your workouts slowly at first and build up over time. Most people have a tendency to overwork their bodies and this can lead to injuries. Learn to listen to your body. You should become familiar with how your body responds to weight training and aerobic exercise. Once you have established how much you can lift, set a realistic goal to increase the weight over a period of time. Some trainers recommend keeping a workout journal to monitor your progress.

Gaining muscle mass in a specific area requires training with weights to apply tension to that muscle. The muscle fibers will respond by growing, or going into "hypertrophy." Over the course of time, increasing weights will increase muscle size. Once you have achieved the desired effects, maintaining muscle size requires regular weight training in that muscle group. Most trainers recommend exercising one or two muscle groups in a workout session, for example biceps and triceps on the first day, followed by back, chest, shoulders, and legs. It may be advisable, for instance, to alternate workouts with abdominal crunches and aerobic exercise three times a week. Most body-builders do very little, if any, aerobic exercise because this has a tendency to diminish muscle size.

Aerobic exercise is very important, especially as you age, because it improves your overall cardio-pulmonary performance. Once you have established your goal weight and you are content with the amount of lean body mass you have achieved, it is appropriate to add aerobic exercise to your program. It is recommended that you introduce about twenty to thirty minutes of aerobic exercise a week using a treadmill, the elliptical machine, or the stationary bicycle, preferably on an empty stomach to increase fat loss. You can alternate machines with aerobics classes, jogging, or riding a bicycle when the weather permits. Ultimately, the most efficient way to improve muscle tone, increase cardio-pulmonary performance, and increase metabolism is through physical activity like sports, such as volleyball, tennis, and swimming.

Maintaining muscle requires energy. To build a lean healthy body requires eating right. Depriving yourself of food does not result in weight loss. When you starve yourself, your body catches on, and quickly compensates by slowing down your metabolism. Energy is then mobilized from lean muscle, the same muscle you have worked so hard to gain. The result is a tired, weak body that has a suppressed immune system as a result of inadequate nutritional intake. In addition, hungry people are very cranky. The best way to lose weight is to maintain a healthy diet that is high in protein and low in carbohydrates. Carbohydrates are like Chinese food. They are delicious, addicting, and in twenty minutes you want more. Protein requires more energy to metabolize and as a result it sustains you for longer periods of time.

Protein-rich foods include chicken and turkey; fish, such as salmon, tuna, and snapper, are also high in protein, except when deep-fried. The number one source for protein is egg whites, which are very popular for weight trainers; however, avoid the yolk, which is high in cholesterol. Red meats are also a good source of protein. Contrary to popular belief, lean cuts of sirloin, round, and chuck have less then 7 percent fat.

Since most people argue that their diet is adequate, try keeping a food journal for twenty-four hours. Write

Dr. Frank's Tips on How to Trim Down

1. Limit your intake of alcohol, fruit juice, and carbonated sodas. They're high in sugar and sodium, which can lead to water retention.
2. Drink plenty of water.
3. Eat six smaller nutritious meals a day. This will keep your metabolism revved up and will burn more calories.
4. Try to eat protein-rich meals instead of complex carbohydrates.
5. When in doubt, avoid all things white: sugar, flour, salt, and rice. It's better to stick with whole grains and unrefined food sources.

Ages at which specific diagnostic or preventative measures are appropriate

AGE	20–30	31–39	40–49	50–60	61+
ANNUAL PHYSICAL (HEIGHT, WEIGHT, BP, TEMP, URINE, CBC, CHEMISTRIES, LIPIDS, VISION, AND HEARING	YES	YES	YES	YES	YES
STD/HIV SCREENING	YES	YES	YES	YES	YES
RECTAL	NO	NO	YES	YES	YES
PSA	NO	NO	YES	YES	YES
COLONOSCOPY	NO	NO	NO	YES	YES
TETANUS SHOT EVERY TEN YEARS	YES	YES	YES	YES	YES
HEPATITIS A/B VACCINE	YES	YES	YES	YES	YES
PPD ANNUALLY	YES	YES	YES	YES	YES
SMOKING, ALCOHOL, DRUG ASSESSMENT	YES	YES	YES	YES	YES
MENTAL HEALTH ASSESSMENT	YES	YES	YES	YES	YES

down everything you eat and the time at which it was consumed. Afterward, review the journal with your doctor to see exactly what your diet consists of.

Maintaining a routine diet and exercise regimen is a great way to keep in shape. Do not get obsessed with weight itself. It's better to rely on how well your clothes fit then an actual number.

Finally, no gay health assessment would be complete without a thorough review of how you envision yourself. Gay men are particularly prone to issues concerning body image. Body Dysmorphic Disorder (BDD) is an unhealthy preoccupation with one's appearance that can interfere with daily life, creating anxiety and depression. The result is a compulsive concern over the slightest defect in one's own appearance. This can lead to eating disorders, anabolic steroids use, and plastic surgery.

CHAPTER 4

Sexually Transmitted Diseases

GONORRHEA IS caused by the bacterium *Neisseria gonorrhoeae,* and infects the urethra in men. Gonorrhea and her sister chlamydia are closely related organisms and are the most common causes of curable STDs in men. Also known as the "clap," gonorrhea can infect the rectum, the throat, and, rarely, the conjunctiva, the membrane that lines the eyelid and eye surface. Once a person is infected with gonorrhea, he can transmit the organism even without having symptoms. People are considered contagious until they have been treated. About half of those infected don't even have symptoms. When symptoms do occur, they are often within two to ten days after exposure, but can take up to thirty days and include the following:

> *painful urination*
> *anal itching or bleeding*
> *sore throat*
> *greenish yellow or whitish discharge from the urethra.*
> *painful or swollen testicles*

Risk factors include multiple sex partners and unprotected sex. Gonorrhea is a very common infectious disease. In the United States each year, about 700,000 people are infected with gonorrhea, and about 75 percent of all reported cases are found in younger persons aged fifteen to twenty-nine. Diagnosing gonorrhea can be made by swabbing the urethral discharge and having it sent to the lab for analysis. Most patients wince at the idea of having their urethra swabbed, but now there is a special urine test to detect the presence of both gonorrhea and chlamydia.

In the 1980s, gonorrhea became resistant to penicillin and tetracycline. As a result, the CDC recommended fluoroquinolone antibiotics as the treatment for gonorrhea. The oral medication ciprofloxacin revolutionized the treatment of gonorrhea; however, the number of cases of fluoroquinolone-resistant gonorrhea has more than doubled between 2002 and 2003.

"The drug-resistant strain is a rapidly emerging health concern for gay and bisexual men," said Dr. John Douglas, the CDC's STD prevention director. This was an alarming statement made in April 2004 because the rates of drug-resistant gonorrhea in gay and bisexual men were twelve times higher than in straight men. The number of drug-resistant cases increased from 1.8 percent in 2002 to 4.9 percent in 2003. This was in contrast to the increase in cases in straight men from 0.2 percent to 0.4 percent.

The increased prevalence of this strain appears to be concentrated in the Pacific Islands (Hawaii) and California; however, the New York City health department reported twenty-two cases of fluoroquinolone-resistant gonorrhea from January to July 2003 after identifying only eight cases in 2002. Officials theorized that infected men from the West Coast had then traveled to other areas. More proof that resistant strains were making their way across the U.S. emerged when a cluster of twelve patients with decreased susceptibility to azithromycin, another commonly used drug, was found in Kansas City.

"There is mounting evidence these increasing STD rates are fueled by a variety of factors," said Dr. Douglas, "including relaxed safe-sex practices, substance abuse, crystal methamphetamine use, and the availability of the Internet for meeting sex partners." This claim is supported by parallel increases in syphilis and HIV. The CDC recommends that doctors not use a fluoroquinolone antibiotic in gay and bisexual men but recommends using an injectable antibiotic like ceftriaxone. The drug resistant strain appears to still be sensitive to this form of injectable antibiotic. In routine cases, treatment can include the oral medication, azithromycin, which is also acceptable.

If unsuccessfully treated gonorrhea can cause epididymitis, a painful condition of the testicles that can sometimes lead to infertility. Without prompt treatment, gonorrhea can also affect the prostate (prostatitis) and lead to scarring inside the urethra, making urination difficult. In some cases, gonorrhea can spread to the blood or joints. This condition can be life-threatening. It has also been suggested that men with recurrent gonorrhea are at higher risk for contracting HIV, and those men who have both HIV and gonorrhea are likelier to transmit HIV.

Chlamydia is caused by *Chlamydia trachomatis* and is one of the most common sexually transmitted diseases. This infection is easily spread because it often has no associated symptoms and may be unknowingly passed to sexual partners. In fact, about 50 percent of men who contract chlamydia are without any symptoms. Since it is such a silent STD, detection is not always so easy. Usually a diagnosis is made after a routine STD screening or after you've been made aware that your partner has been infected. When symptoms do occur, they usually begin within one to three weeks of contact and can include the following:

> *Small amounts of clear or cloudy discharge from the tip of the penis*
> *Painful urination*
> *Burning and itching around the opening of the penis*
> *Pain and swelling around the testicles*

Like gonorrhea, chlamydia is diagnosed with either a urethral swab or a urine sample. Typically, everyone should be treated when they present with the above symptoms. It is common practice to treat for both organisms at the same time, and abstinence from sexual activity for at least one week is strongly advised. All recent sexual partners should be made aware of your diagnosis. Treatment consists of either a single dose of azithromycin or a week of doxycycline (twice daily.) Consequences of untreated chlamydia are almost the same as for gonorrhea.

Syphilis, also known as the Great Mimicker among physicians, is a sexually transmitted disease that has been the source of much debate among doctors and historians who still argue about the timing and whereabouts of its origin. It first made its appearance in Europe in 1495, which coincidentally correlated with the return of soldiers who had participated in the wars of that period. Some even accused Columbus of bringing back the disease from the New World when he returned to Europe.

Regardless of its origin, syphilis has remained a constant presence throughout history, and its contagious properties reside in an organism called *Treponema pallidum,* a type of bacterium called a spirochete. Syphilis is a highly infectious disease spread primarily by sexual activity, including oral and anal sex. On occasion, the disease can be passed from one infected man to his partner through prolonged kissing or close body contact. Although this disease is spread from sores, the vast majority of cases go unrecognized, and the infected person is often unaware of the disease and unknowingly passes it on.

Syphilis is characterized by three distinct stages.

Primary syphilis: People with primary syphilis develop one or more chancre sores. Chancre (pronounced *shang-ker*) is a shallow-based, painless ulcer that occurs on the genitals or in the mouth somewhere between seven and ninety days from exposure. The chancre typically resolves on its own without treatment, usually within two to six weeks.

Secondary syphilis begins about six weeks after exposure and can even present while the initial chancre is still present. This stage can last for one to three months if left untreated. People with secondary syphilis experience a rash much like that of chickenpox but more typically on the palms of the hands and soles of the feet. Patients also experience headaches, sore throat, joint pain, and muscle aches. Sometimes moist lesions develop in the groin or as whitish patches in the mouth. These teem with spirochetes and are highly infectious even through kissing. Like primary syphilis, secondary syphilis can resolve without treatment; however, patients do remain infectious.

Tertiary, or *late-stage, syphilis* progresses if the infection is left untreated. This stage is characterized by problems affecting the cardiovascular system, causing heart-valve damage or aneurysms. It can also affect the central nervous system with *neurosyphilis,* which is characterized by softening of the brain tissues, causing progressive paralysis, dementia, and death.

Syphilis is diagnosed by a blood test called the rapid plasma regain, or RPR, which is confirmed by a fluorescent treponema antibody test, or FTA. To diagnose tertiary syphilis, a spinal tap (lumbar puncture) may be required.

Treatment for primary and secondary syphilis is with injectable penicillin. For tertiary syphilis, especially in the HIV population, intravenous penicillin is the treatment of choice.

Men account for over 95 percent of the cases of primary and secondary syphilis. Of those men interviewed in New York City by the board of health, MSMs made up most of the population, and half of those men also said they were HIV positive. Syphilis facilitates HIV transmission and men should be screened routinely. Similar outbreaks among MSMs were also noted in other cities like Los Angeles, San Francisco, Seattle, Miami, Atlanta, and Houston.

Syphilis is spread through direct contact with skin, especially during the secondary phase, or through contact with an open sore or lesion. Usually, contact occurs during anal or oral sex, but syphilis can even be spread through kissing if there are sores in the mouth. It is vital that if you are diagnosed with syphilis that you should warn all recent partners. Likewise, if a sex partner informs you of his diagnosis of syphilis, then you should get checked by a doctor even if it was one year ago or longer.

Herpes is a virus that causes vesicular blebs or blisters that "pop up" like pimples. These nasty eruptions show up at the most unsuitable times, like before a big date or prior to a business presentation, and in the most inappropriate places—genitals, lips, and anus. Stress can induce an eruption of herpes, and the only recourse a man has is to flee to his doctor for some help!

Herpes usually appears as blister-like lesions on the mouth, which are typically herpes type I, or sores on the genitals, which is herpes type II. That is not to say that a lesion found on the mouth has to be herpes type I, and only lesions of the genitals have to be herpes type II. It all depends on the mode of transmission and who was doing what to whom. A male with herpes type I lesions on his lips is contagious, and if he performs oral sex on you, then you can inherit the type I virus on your genitals. The same goes for the opposite—that is, passing herpes type II from your genitals to someone's mouth.

Common terms for herpes include "cold sore" or "fever blister." These painful papules can drive you insane once they rear their ugly head, and usually someone with a history of herpes can tell when one is coming on because of an annoying tingling sensation that develops at the site of eruption. Men with active herpes lesions are

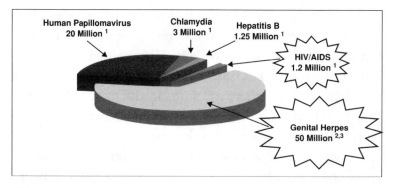

The Prevalence of Genital Herpes in the U.S.
There are over 1 million genital herpes infections per year in the U.S.
[1] Centers for Disease Control and Prevention. Available at:
   http://www.cdc.gov. Accessed November 14, 2006.
[2] Xu F, et al. *JAMA* 2006; 296:964-973.
[3] U.S. Census Bureau. Available at http://www.census.gov. Accessed
   December 12, 2006.

considered contagious and they should warn you about
that. That is why you shouldn't kiss anyone on the mouth
who has a "fever blister" or engage in sexual activity if
they have any active lesions on their penis or anus.

The CDC estimates that there are over one million
new cases of genital herpes each year in the United States.
Genital herpes is the most prevalent STD in the United
States with an estimated one in five adults infected. When
clinicians speak of genital herpes, they are referring to
herpes type 2 (HSV-2). HSV-2 is a sexually transmitted
disease that often causes no visible symptoms, and it is
possible to contract genital herpes from someone who has
no symptoms at all. The majority of cases of HSV-2 transmission are due to this type of asymptomatic viral shed-
ding.

For the initial outbreak of HSV-2, the time from exposure to the initial presentation can be up to two weeks.
Some patients develop flulike symptoms. Blisters may

develop on your genitals or anus. Within a few days the blisters will break and ooze. These sores will usually heal within three weeks without treatment. During the time these sores begin to heal you are extremely infectious and susceptible to HIV if exposed.

There are cases of people who develop HSV (types 1 and 2) and never have a recurrent outbreak. Usually patients develop a recurrence if they are exposed to stress, fatigue, and other infections. If you have never been diagnosed with HSV, and you develop suspicious ulcerations or sores, then you should see a health-care provider. HSV can be diagnosed by physical exam, culture, and blood test to detect HSV antibodies in the blood. Once you've been diagnosed with HSV, there are various antiviral medications that your doctor can prescribe to provide relief of symptoms and speed up recovery. Antiviral medication like acyclovir, famciclovir, and valacyclovir are commonly prescribed to treat initial and recurrent outbreaks of HSV. Also there are over-the-counter nonsteroidal anti-inflammatories that can provide relief from the pain of the ulcerations. Topical creams, however, are not made for the treatment of genital herpes.

Currently, the CDC recommends "suppressive therapy" (that means taking antiviral medication daily for one year or more) in patients who have frequent outbreaks of genital herpes. Daily treatment not only decreases the rate of recurrent outbreaks, but it also decreases the likelyhood of transmission to your sexual partner. However, despite being on suppressive therapy, patients can still have outbreaks. So be sure to contact your doctor if you feel you are having an outbreak while on antiviral medication. This is especially important to consider if you are HIV positive, because an impaired immune system makes you more susceptible to future outbreaks. HIV positive men who have several outbreaks a year should be on suppressive therapy indefinitely.

In 2007, the CDC defined the synergistic relationship between genital herpes and HIV as a syndemic. The relationship between these two viruses adversely affects both people at risk of HIV and those who are already HIV positive. Simply put, genital herpes is fueling the fire of the AIDS epidemic. It is known that a significant proportion of HIV infections in the United States can be attributed to HSV-2. Studies show that HSV-2 significantly increases the risk of acquiring HIV due to mucosal barrier breakdown, which increases susceptibility to HIV. Based on this evidence, it is important that men who have sex with men get screened routinely for all STDs, including HSV-2, especially if they are HIV positive.

For a discussion of *Human Papilloma Virus* (HPV), please see the section on "male Pap smear" (pp. 25–29).

Hepatitis is a viral infection that causes inflammation of the liver. There are other causes of hepatitis, but this section will discuss only the viral forms that are transmitted through sexual contact. The three most common forms of hepatitis are lettered A, B, and C.

Hepatitis A is a virus that is transmitted through fecal-oral contamination. Usually we ingest something that has been contaminated with fecal material containing the virus. The most common scenario is ingesting contaminated water and food sources, as in a restaurant. Your little cutie waiter who unknowingly has the virus forgets to wash his hands in the bathroom and subsequently touches your chicken paillard—and bang! You have gotten more than a meal. Gay men usually contract hepatitis A through oral-anal sex, or what is commonly referred to as rimming. Hepatitis A is a short-term illness that usually resolves on its own without long-term consequences.

After exposure to hepatitis A, symptoms usually develop two to six weeks later. They are usually mild and often mimic the "stomach flu," with fever, body aches, abdominal pain, nausea, and a slight yellow tinge to the eyes (icterus) and skin (jaundice.) You are contagious during this period and can transmit the virus through contact with your stool. Symptoms usually last less than two months and there is no medical treatment for hepatitis A. The best thing to do is get plenty of rest and stay hydrated in order to avoid dehydration. Ten days into the disease, your body will develop antibodies to hepatitis A. Once you have this antibody you will be immune from ever contracting hepatitis A again. Currently, there is a hepatitis A vaccine available. I offer it to all my gay male patients in order to prevent them from developing this disease, especially those who are HIV positive. The vaccine is covered by most insurance and is given in two separate injections six months apart.

Hepatitis B is another type of virus that causes inflammation of the liver. Unlike hepatitis A, hepatitis B is a more complex disease. For one, it is transmitted through blood and body fluids like semen. Hepatitis B is usually a self-limiting disease, which means that most patients go through the infection within three to six months. Approximately, one third of those infected have no symptoms, but those who do present like hepatitis A, with fever, nausea, vomiting, jaundice, and body aches. In most cases symptoms resolve and immunity is established due to the development of the hepatitis B antibody. Some people are not so lucky. In 5 to 10 percent of cases, those who contract hepatitis B will go on to become chronic carriers. Patients who show signs of persistent infection beyond six months are considered carriers. This means you are still contagious and can transmit the virus to other men through unprotected sex. As a carrier, you are still prone to the effects of the virus on your liver. There is a small chance that the virus will go away in a percentage of patients who are carriers. For the most part these patients will become chronic carriers.

Chronic hepatitis B is a disease that involves progressive damage to the liver, which can ultimately lead to cirrhosis. Cirrhosis is scarring of the liver so that bloodflow to the liver is impaired; this leads to build up of fluid in the body and failure of the liver cells to function. It is estimated that men who have sex with men are ten times more likely to contract hepatitis B than the general population. So how do you avoid contracting it?

1. Always use condoms during anal sex.
2. Get vaccinated.
3. Do not share toothbrushes, razors, or nail clippers with other men.
4. Avoid biting and coming into contact with open sores or blood.
5. Be careful of tattoo parlors, and ensure that a new needle is used if you get a tattoo.

When a person first becomes infected with hepatitis B, he may develop fever, fatigue, nausea, jaundice, and abdominal pain anytime between six weeks to six months from the time of exposure. However, it is possible to contract hepatitis B and pass the virus without ever having any symptoms. Usually a doctor detects the hepatitis B antibody on a routine screening. If this happens to you, consider yourself very lucky. It is estimated that 30 percent of those infected will not show any signs or symptoms of hepatitis B.

Diagnosis of hepatitis B by your doctor usually involves a thorough physical exam and blood tests to assess liver function. The diagnosis is confirmed with detection of viral antibodies in the blood. Post-exposure prophylaxis is indicated for individuals who have been exposed to hepatitis B within less than two weeks. In these cases patients are given a dose of the hepatitis B vaccine and hepatitis B immune globulin. The second and third doses of the vaccine are given at their usual intervals of one and six months later. In 95 percent of these cases protection against hepatitis B is estimated.

For patients who have exceeded the two-week limit I recommend bed rest and hydration. Some doctors recommend maintaining a high-calorie diet despite symptoms of nausea, and to also avoid alcohol or anything else that might stress your liver, like acetaminophen, or Tylenol. As for herbal and nutritional supplements, consult your doctor before ingesting. In cases of chronic hepatitis B several combinations of drugs are available. These are:

> *Interferon: an injection that is given for at least six months*
> *Epivir: an antiviral medication*
> *Hepsera: this drug works well in people whose disease doesn't respond to epivir, but in high doses it can cause kidney problems*
> *Baraclude and Tyzeka: These are the newest drugs for hepatitis B.*

If your disease becomes chronic, a liver biopsy (tissue sample) may be obtained to determine the severity.

A liver biopsy is also useful in monitoring the progression of liver disease and to diagnose cirrhosis. Individuals with chronic hepatitis B, especially those with cirrhosis, are at an increased risk of developing hepatocellular carcinoma, or primary liver cancer. Although this type of cancer is relatively rare in the United States, the fact remains that hepatitis B can result in cancer. Fortunately, there is now a combination hepatitis A and B vaccine available; it is administered, like the hepatitis B vaccine, three times over six months.

Hepatitis C is the third in a line of viral infections affecting the liver. Its effect on the gay community has been aggressive because co-infection rates with HIV have been increasing.

Hepatitis C is a complicated virus. First there are at least six different subtypes, and each responds differently to treatment. In the United States, type 1 is the most common and the hardest to treat. Although hepatitis C is not efficiently transmitted sexually, there is a correlation with persons at risk for infection through injection drug use who seek care at STD clinics and HIV facilities. The recreational drug crystal methamphetamine has certainly made its presence known in the gay community. This epidemic in and of itself has increased the incidence of unprotected sex and subsequent rise in hepatitis B as well as HIV.

Hepatitis C has affected nearly four million Americans. Although most patients have no symptoms at the onset, some do develop jaundice, nausea, vomiting, flu-like symptoms, and malaise. Diagnosis of hepatitis C is made through a blood test to detect the antibody, which usually appears within a few weeks after exposure. Hepatitis C can be a self-limiting disease in 15 to 45 percent of the cases, but most statistics show that chronic infec-

JOHN, a forty-year-old lawyer, contracted hepatitis C after sharing needles with a hustler one night. I had been treating John's HIV for the past three years when we discovered the virus on a routine physical exam. John did not disclose the incident with the hustler until after he was told about his hepatitis C diagnosis. He had been in recovery for drugs and alcohol for nearly three years and this was his first relapse.

After the initial workup, John was enrolled in treatment. He had to guarantee that he would make routine visits in order for me to monitor his blood counts and to assess how well he was tolerating the medication regimen. As with any viral hepatitis, patients are strongly discouraged from ingesting alcohol or any medications that are potentially toxic to the liver. Always use condoms when engaging in sexual activity, and don't share needles, toothbrushes, or razors. Currently, there is no vaccine available to prevent hepatitis C. As part of his treatment, John was also vaccinated against hepatitis A and B.

tion develops in 75 to 85 percent of people infected. In those cases work up includes blood test to check:

> *Serum chemistries*
> *Liver-function tests*
> *Complete blood counts*
> *Hepatitis C viral load*
> *Hepatitis C genotype*

In addition to these blood tests, people are referred for ultrasound of their liver and to a gastroenterologist for a liver biopsy for staging. Treatment for hepatitis C is complicated and currently consists of pegylated interferon and ribavirin. Interferon is given as a weekly injection for approximately forty-eight weeks, administered with oral ribavirin daily. The virus is eliminated through treatment in about 25 percent of cases with hepatitis C, type 1. The side effects from this combination therapy are numerous and range from:

> *Flu-like symptoms*
> *Depression and suicidal thoughts*
> *Low blood counts, especially anemia*
> *Chronic fatigue*

Pubic lice, or "crabs," are flat, millimeter-length nits that are contracted through close contact. They actually look like crabs under a magnifying glass but can be seen with the naked eye. These lice burrow into the skin, usually around the pubic region or anywhere there is hair. They feed off blood and cause intense itching. Patients usually present with reddish marks on their skin and excoriations secondary to nail marks from repetitive scratching. Sometimes eggs or whitish blebs can be seen attached to hair follicles. Typically, patients present with complaints of rash and intense itching in the region of the groin, armpits, and anal region. Lice can actually be picked off with fingers or removed with a comb. Doctors usually diagnose crabs with physical symptoms, and prescribe treatment with an application of permethrin that is put on from head to toe, avoiding the eyes, nose, and mouth region. The patient is instructed to sleep with the medication on and then rinse it off in the morning. All sheets, towels, and clothing need to be washed, and it is important that all close contacts be made aware and treated as well so as to avoid re-infection.

Scabies, although very similar to pubic lice, are a different mite that also burrows into the outer layers of the skin. They are much smaller than crabs and burrow underneath the skin to lay their eggs. Often they can be felt in between fingers and toes, in the web portion of the skin. Itchy, irritated skin develops in the infested area with short wavy lines produced by the burrowing action of the scabies mite. Scabies are also transmitted through close contact with a man who has scabies or by lying on his infested bed or couch. Scabies can even be contracted from a toilet seat. Prevention and treatment is the same as for pubic lice.

Parasites are organisms that grow and feed off of another organism. If these critters enter the digestive tract, they can cause symptoms similar to those of food poisoning. You can contract parasites and amoebas the same way the hepatitis A virus is contracted—through fecal-oral contamination. Rimming, the act of stimulating your partner's anus with your tongue, is a common way gay men contract parasites.

A variety of organisms can make their home in the colon: giardia, salmonella, shigella, blastocystis, or campylobacter, but most are usually dealt with by the body's natural defense system. There is, however, always the possibility that once you are infected by one of these organisms you might develop a full-blown case of dysentery. Dysentery is another name for gastroenteritis, or the stomach flu. It is not always certain that if you come into contact with one of these organisms you will definitely fall prey to gastroenteritis. It depends on your body's immune function and how much of the organism you were exposed to. Let's say, for example, that you are feeling tired and stressed out because of work; your immune system is down, but your boyfriend is on a natural high, having been offered a new promotion. If you were both to be exposed to giardia then, you would be more susceptible to a bout then he would be. It is also possible that if you were to become infected, you could transmit the parasite to him, especially if he enjoys rimming you. Risk of infection is always increased with repeated exposure to the offending organism.

Giardiasis is an intestinal illness caused by the parasite, *Giardia lamblia,* also known as *Giardia intestinalis.* It is one of the most common parasites that affect gay men. The symptoms of giardia include diarrhea, abdominal cramps, gas, and nausea. Diagnosing intestinal parasites and bacteria is done through a stool culture, which involves collecting your stool with a kit that is provided by your doctor. It's not fun, and it sounds messy, but there are so many different types of parasites, amoebas, and bacteria that proper identification of the organism is essential to choosing the correct medication.

If you have these symptoms, you'll be given a stool kit to use at home, and then you'll be started on two antibiotics to cover both bacterial and parasitic infections. Once the stool culture results come in, doctors can modify the treatment by removing the unnecessary antibiotic. Over-the-counter antidiarrheals are not recommended, even though it is sometimes impossible to function in the real world when you have the trots. Antidiarrheals inhibit your body from naturally ridding itself of the harmful toxins and causative organisms. One of the body's objectives in producing diarrhea is to remove the offending organisms naturally.

As far as STDs are concerned, it is important to understand that although sex can be quite pleasurable, there can be consequences, especially if you have multiple sex partners. Try to remember to recognize any genital symptoms such as discharge, burning during urination, or unusual sores or rashes. This should signal you to stop having sex and to consult a doctor immediately. If you are told you have any STD and receive treatment, you should notify all of your recent sex partners so that they may see a doctor as soon as possible.

PART II

Gay Sex

CHAPTER 5

The Anatomy of Gay Sex

IN MEDICAL SCHOOL, doctors are taught anatomy and physiology. This knowledge is useful as it pertains to sex and health problems arising from sex. Gay men often know very little about their bodies and their bodies' functions. It is important to know that the very nature of gay sex can affect your health. That is why you need to become familiar with the anatomical sites of pleasure and to understand what they do. Once this has been established, it will help in ascertaining why something doesn't seem right.

NIPPLES

Nipples in men, unlike those of women, are considered nonfunctional with regard to lactation. However, the nipple and the surrounding area called the areola have erotic receptors, which qualify them as sex organs. The nipple is made up of muscle cells arranged in a cylindrical fashion. The skin overlying them has a rich nerve supply which is sensitive to both tactile and erotic stimuli. Sexual arousal or manual manipulation can cause the nipples to become erect and this increases their sensitivity.

The basic evolution of the nipple is that it developed along the milk line, which in humans extends from the armpits to the groin. For some men this circuitry is highly sensitive, and that is why some men boast that their penis is "hard-wired" to their nipples. There are even some men who experience rigorous ejaculations with manual stimulation of the nipples during climax. Unfortunately, this is not true for all men.

Clamps, piercings, and other accessories have been known to enhance the stimulation of the nipple. Some men try to increase the sensitivity of their own nipples through progressive manipulation. Repetitive twisting and pulling on the nipple itself will cause the muscles to increase in size, or hypertrophy. Enlarged nipples are said to be highly sensitive, and visually, they can be quite arousing for men who find big nipples a turn-on. There are even various suction devices available that will aid you in enlarging your nipples; however, remember that nipples are delicate and the skin overlying them is prone to chaffing and bleeding, especially after prolonged friction from fingers or facial hair. If you enjoy nipple play, attend to them as you would your lips. If they are dry or chapped, avoid contact and keep the area moist with Vaseline. Allow time for tender nipples to heal before resuming play and monitor them for any signs or symptoms of infection—pain, redness, or swelling. Likewise, do not allow anyone to put his mouth on irritated nipples because the risk for contracting an infection is higher. Remember that a stranger's mouth is not the cleanest part of his body.

Most disorders of the male breast are benign. Gynecomastia is the most common male breast disorder. This is not a tumor but rather an increase in the amount of breast tissue. A man with gynecomastia usually presents with a disklike growth under his nipple and areola, which can be felt. Gynecomastia is a common condition due to changes in hormone balance that usually affects teenage boys and older men. Obesity increases the amount of estrogen and can also result in gynecomastia. Men who use anabolic steroids are also prone to developing abnormal breast tissue due to estrogen. Although men's glands normally produce some estrogen, it is not enough to cause breast growth. Prolonged alcohol use, which can affect the liver, can also result in disproportionate hormone metabolism and this can lead to gynecomastia.

Other common causes of gynecomastia include some commonly prescribed medications like the ones that treat heartburn, high blood pressure, and heart failure. If you develop a lump under your nipple or in the vicinity of the areola, always consult your doctor.

Nipple piercing has been a consistent part of gay culture. An important fact to note about nipple piercings are that they usually involve a slow healing process. It can take up to eight weeks. Before you undergo any piercing, ensure that the technician properly cleans your skin with an alcohol swab first and that a new needle is opened from its packaging before it touches your skin. Contact with a contaminated needle can transmit bacterial infections, hepatitis, and HIV.

After-care for freshly pierced nipples includes keeping them clean and dry. Apply ice packs or a bag of frozen vegetables to sore nipples, or use salt water soaks, for no

THE AMERICAN CANCER Society reports that in 2006 just over 1,700 men were diagnosed with invasive breast cancer. Once a patient called me frantically because he developed a painful lump under his left nipple; he was worried it might be cancer. Upon further investigation, this patient admitted to recently administering anabolic steroids for the past four weeks. Gynecomastia, or "bitch tits" as this patient referred to it, is a common result of anabolic steroid use. Although the breast tissue can regress if the steroids are discontinued, this is not always the case. Sometimes doctors recommend a course of anti-estrogen medication like tamoxifen, which can diminish the size of the abnormal breast tissue. The medications, however, are specified for breast cancer treatment in women and have serious side effects. Often men with gynecomastia have to resort to surgery in order to remove the unwanted tissue.

more then five minutes, to provide relief. Avoid contact with hands and mouths for the first two weeks after the procedure because early manipulation can lead to infection. If your piercing takes longer than two months to heal, you might be experiencing an allergic reaction to the jewelry. This will cause rejection and result in abscess formation and infection. Signs to look for include persistent pain, redness, and discharge. If this is the case, consult your doctor at once.

ARMPITS

The area under the arm that connects to the shoulder is termed the axilla. This is what is commonly referred to as the armpit. In men this area is usually hairy and carries a distinct body odor due to fatty secretions produced by apocrine glands. Most men try to diminish this odor—as it is considered offensive—by washing routinely and wearing antiperspirant or deodorant.

In gay culture, the armpit is considered an erogenous zone and it can be a very sexy part of a man's anatomy. If you subscribe to the leather community or bear lifestyle, a hairy, smelly armpit is very erotic. The musky smell it emits defines a man almost like a natural cologne. You may even enjoy sniffing, licking, and caressing another man's armpit. The dark hidden recesses of a man's axilla are erotic for the same reason someone may enjoy the space between a man's scrotum and his thigh. Axillary eroticism has evolved for some who practice axillary intercourse. This is when a man inserts his penis into another man's armpit in order to achieve orgasm.

Few gay men shave their armpits, although many do trim so that the hair does not extend beyond the armpit area itself. Others enjoy the natural state that their hair grows in.

Medically, common problems associated with the armpit involve ingrown hairs, especially for those who trim or shave this region. As new hairs grow, they can become trapped, and due to the excessive amount of bacteria along with the multiple sebaceous glands, infection is likely. Folliculitis, or infected hair follicles, often present as pain and tenderness in the armpit with associated redness. Pus can also accumulate, as in an abscess or, less discreetly, with multiple pustules. The mainstay of treatment is to keep the area clean and dry. Avoid deodorant, antiperspirants, and heavy perfumes, as they can exacerbate the infection. Treatment usually involves antibiotics and anti-inflammatory creams.

Hidradenitis suppurativa is a disorder of the apocrine glands in the armpits. Plugging of the apocrine duct and hair follicle will result in dilatation and inflammation, which can lead to bacterial growth and infection. The symptoms are usually red, painful, and tender armpits. Sometimes drainage occurs, especially if it is associated with abscess formation. The natural course of this disease is complex. For the most part the condition is able to resolve itself, especially with antibiotics and anti-inflammatory medication. A chronic form does exist, however, which can result in thickening of the skin, called fibrosis, and sinus tract formation with persistent drainage. In this case, surgical intervention may be required.

Gay men who use anabolic steroids, as well as HIV-positive men, are also at risk for developing enlarged lymph nodes in the armpits. Firm, round, immobile lesions should be examined by a physician. Although cancer should be ruled out, this condition can have other multiple medical causes.

THE PENIS

There is a wonderful line in *Peggy Sue Got Married,* when Peggy's mother confronts her daughter about her recent odd behavior. She asks, "Peggy, do you know what a penis is? Well, then stay away from it." That line resonates—and for good reason—because Peggy's mother was warning her daughter about the power of the penis.

The relationship between a man and his member is a unique one. The penis has been known to have a mind of its own, and this makes for a highly interesting marriage. Sometimes they agree, sometimes they disagree, but the bottom line is that neither can survive without the other. Since the dawn of man, the penis has been the source of controversy. For centuries men have blamed their poor judgment on their genitals, especially when it concerns crimes of passion.

Puberty is defined as the age in which a boy transforms into adulthood. Through the development of the testicles triggered by the brain to produce a surge of testosterone, the penis becomes engorged with blood and swells to its full size. In the beginning, the penis does this without provocation. Regardless of social situation, etiquette, or concern for embarrassment, the penis acts as its own boss. As a boy matures, he learns how to manage his penis, and the reward for this great partnership is a glorious outcome—the orgasm. Masturbation becomes a ritual for boys. Finding private times in a locked bathroom can became a religious experience. Since puberty is such a defining cornerstone in every boy's life, young gay boys are often confused when they realize that the object of their desire is the same sex.

Physiologically, the penis is an extraordinary organ because it serves a dual purpose—the evacuation of

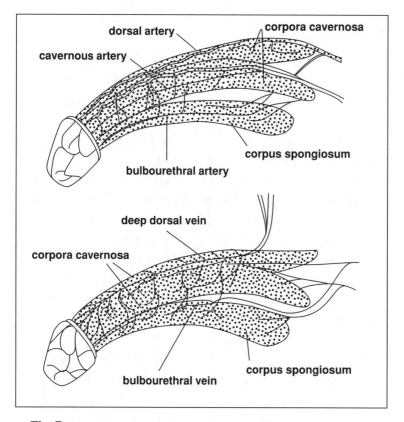

The Penis

urine and the ejaculation of semen. Anatomically, the penis is formed by a spongy corpus spongiosum that is covered by skin. It has its own nerve supply, artery, and veins. Also running through the shaft is the urethra, which acts as the conduit for both semen and urine. This is a truly unique design because the mechanism by which flow is established is controlled by an involuntarily process in the brain. That's why we can't piss and cum at the same time. A thin elastic skin loosely connects the penis and extends over the head in uncircumcised men. This is called the foreskin and is the source of pleasure for many men who enjoy contact with an uncut man.

In 2005, the NIH reported that circumcision reduced a man's risk of contracting HIV by half. Uncircumcised men are more susceptible to infection because the underside of their foreskin is rich in Langerhans cells, which easily attach to the virus. Since the foreskin often suffers tears during sexual intercourse, this allows for the virus's entry into the bloodstream.

Care for the foreskin involves cleansing the underside with water daily to avoid buildup of smegma—the waxy collection of cells, oils, and bacteria that develop under the foreskin. The characteristic "cheesy" appearance also has a distinct odor. The bacteria, *Mycobacterium smegmatis*, which makes up smegma, can cause balanitis, or severe irritation of the glans penis.

Since penises come in all sizes and shapes, their uniqueness is as varied as the men they are attached to. Penis talk is common among gay men, and the size and width of a penis can be an obsession for some, hence the name *size queen*. But what is it about a large erection or a big cock that makes some gay men go crazy? The curiosity over penis size has been studied for decades. In fact, Alfred Kinsey had thousands of men measure their own penis, and he found that the results did not correlate with stereotypic myths. Neither race nor the size of a man's foot, hand, or nose corresponded to the length of his penis. In fact, the average penis is between five and seven inches long, measuring from the tip of the head to where the penis inserts into the abdomen. Likewise, the circumference averages about five inches around.

So what is this obsession with size? Psychologists say that a preoccupation with penis size might suggest an underlying insecurity over one's manhood. In gay culture concern over masculinity sometimes gets correlated with the size of a penis. The misconception that only "real men" have big dicks is common. Once again, internalized homophobia gets brought to light when gay men objectify their masculinity by assigning it to a physical attribute.

In contrast, there is a condition known as "micropenis" in which the penis measures less than two inches long. Regardless of actual size, I have known men who were very concerned with the size of their penis, and this resulted in varying degrees of depression. In an attempt to correct this, some have consulted with surgeons about penile enlargement surgery or penis pump devices. The truth is that they do not work. Other procedures like ligamental surgery or fat injection have had minor success. Find a doctor that has experience. Most times patients get disappointed with their outcome because they did not have a realistic expectation. Talk to your doctor before you invest your time and money.

Medical issues concerning the penis are common and a source of great distress for gay men. Some of the more common afflictions include balanitis and phimosis. Balanitis is an inflammation of the penile glans and is particularly significant in the uncircumcised male. If the foreskin is retracted over the swollen glands, it can act as a tourniquet compressing the veins and causing further swelling. Balanitis occurs most commonly in uncircumcised men, especially those with poor hygiene. Inflammation can occur if the sensitive skin under the foreskin is not washed regularly. Sweat and bacteria can collect under the foreskin and this leads to irritation. The presence of tight foreskin may make it difficult to keep this area clean and result in foul-smelling smegma that can accumulate under the foreskin. In addition to Mycobacterium smegmatis, infection with the yeast *Candida albicans* can result in an itchy, red rash. Certain sexually transmitted diseases, including gonorrhea, herpes, and syphilis, can also produce symptoms of balanitis. Men with co-existing medical problems like diabetes are at an even greater risk for balanitis, especially due to the susceptibility to fungal infections. If there is an infection, treatment should include the appropriate antibiotic or antifungal medication. In severe or persistent cases of inflammation, a circumcision may be required. Taking appropriate hygienic measures may also help prevent future bouts of balanitis. Retract the foreskin daily, adequately clean the head with water, and dry. Avoid strong soaps that may cause irritation of the skin.

Phimosis is another condition that affects the foreskin, making it unable to be fully retracted past the head of the penis. This is usually a problem in infants but does exist in adult males. One common cause is chronic balanitis. Phimosis can be painful and uncomfortable, especially during sex. Treatment usually involves surgery, with either a traditional circumcision or the alternative called preputioplasty. This relieves the constricted band of skin with a surgical slit. In some cases, topical steroids work well for milder cases of phimosis. Some doctors recommend stretching the foreskin manually under the guidance of a urologist. The issue here is that if the foreskin is pulled back but then is unable to be passed over the glans penis in its natural position, this will result in a condition known as paraphimosis. It is important that the foreskin be pulled over the glans by using a lubricant and pressing the head of the penis with your fingers so that the blood is drained out. If this doesn't work, seek emergency medical care.

Another more familiar but equally frightening medical condition is called *hematospermia*. This is when a man ejaculates, and there is blood mixed in with his semen. Most cases of hematospermia occur after masturbation or intercourse but are benign and usually self-limiting. The first time this occurs can be a horrifying experience. Men often call their doctor frantically, worried that they have cancer. The origin of the bleed is traumatic rupture of any of the many blood vessels that supply the prostate and the seminal vesicles. This can occur without cause. Most men with hematospermia are in their 30s, and the problem almost always resolves spontaneously, usually within several weeks. Men that have persistent hematospermia for longer than three weeks should undergo evaluation with a urologist to identify the specific cause. Causes can include infection of the prostate and, in rare cases, cancer. Blood in the urine also qualifies for a complete urological evaluation.

Skin manifestations on the penis are also common. Psoriasis appears as thickened plaques with a scaly surface. Although it more commonly affects the knees, elbows, and scalp, the cause is an abnormality of skin production. Psoriasis is a hereditary disorder, and treatment involves topical steroid creams. Eczema, another skin disorder that can affect the penis, is considered a skin reaction to an irritant. Eczema appears as diffuse plaques with a finely scaled surface. In contrast to psoriasis, eczema is very irritating. Other causes of eczema include infection or exposure to chemicals. Also known as dermatitis, it is alleviated with topical steroids.

Penile cancer is a rare condition that occurs when abnormal cells divide and grow. The exact cause of penile cancer is unknown, but there are certain risk factors for the disease, such as being uncircumcised or having HPV.

Symptoms of penile cancer include growths or sores on the penis, abnormal discharge, and bleeding. Surgery to remove the cancer is the most common treatment.

Although not very common, Peyronie's disease is frightening for some men. It occurs in about 1 percent of men between the ages of forty-five and sixty. First described by Francois de la Peyronie, a French surgeon in 1743, this disease involves a deformity of the erect penis. It is characterized by the formation of a hard plaque in the shaft of the penis, causing pain, curvature, and distortion of the penis. The result is excruciating pain during intercourse. In some cases, the pain from Peyronie's disease will resolve over time; however, the curvature usually persists. Since each case differs, most doctors will take a wait-and-see approach. Treatment options include injections of the plaques or surgery.

Another deformity of the penis, known as a fractured penis, involves traumatic rupture of the corpus cavernosum. The term is a misnomer since there is no bone in the penis to break. The name alludes to the fact that the erect penis is like a plastic tube that bends under pressure. This usually occurs during rough insertive anal sex. During intercourse an audible "pop" or "crack" can be heard. Soon afterward, the penis will become flaccid and then begin to swell painfully. The skin overlying the penis will bruise and turn black and blue. Then the shaft of the penis will deviate to the side opposite the injury. For example, if the left corpus cavernosum is ruptured, the penis will be deviated to the right. Serious injury can result in rupture of the urethra. If this happens you will experience blood in the urine. You should apply ice packs to the area and seek immediate medical attention. Medical management consists of cold compresses, pressure dressings, and anti-inflammatory medication. The majority of cases, however, require surgical intervention, which is the most effective form of treatment.

Genital piercing has been widely adopted by gay culture, partly due to the grand claims that it enhances sexual pleasure for both partners. The Prince Albert, or PA, signifies the most common male genital piercing, which involves penetrating the penis from the outside at the frenulum, and then through the urethra. PAs heal more quickly than many other piercings because the area has a rich blood supply and the skin is relatively elastic. Some have even suggested that the sterile urine passing over the PA contributes to the healing process. Infections with the Prince Albert are relatively rare. Initial healing typically takes one to two weeks, with full recovery taking up to nine months or more.

Common misconceptions about the PA are that it is very painful. Most men state that although the area is highly sensitive, the procedure is less painful than other piercings. Some have also cautioned that penetrating the urethra causes dribbling of urine and necessitates sitting down to void. In fact it is not the disruption to the urethra that contributes to the abnormal stream. It is likely to be caused by the piercing itself, which interrupts the flow of urine. Another cause of abnormal urination is when men downsize the gauge of their PA. This leaves a larger hole for urine to flow out of. Some worry about how the PA affects sexual performance. For the most part, the consensus is that it greatly enhances sexual pleasure for both partners. Also do not wear tight-fitting condoms with a large PA in order to avoid tears in the latex.

Controversy exists over the origin of the name Prince Albert. Some allege that Prince Albert of Saxe-Coburg-Gotha, who was Queen Victoria's consort, wore a ring

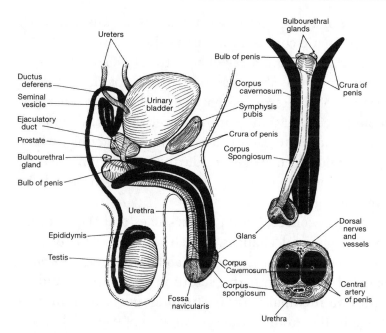

Anatomy of the Normal Male Lower Torso

attached to his penis that was strapped to his thigh. This was in order to maintain the smooth line of his tight pants that were in fashion at the time. Others have remarked that his penis was unusually long and had to be secured so that it would not appear vulgar. There is no evidence, however, to corroborate this legend. Regardless, Queen Victoria and Prince Albert had nine children, and when he died suddenly of typhoid at the early age of forty-two, she was said to be inconsolable. Who could blame her?

TESTICLES AND SCROTUM

In describing the male genitalia it is appropriate to always include the testicles along with the penis. The testicles are twin ovoid-shaped organs that produce sperm and the male sex hormone testosterone. Suspended by the spermatic cord, they are housed in a unique location called the scrotum, a bag of skin that is suspended as an extension of the abdomen. The reason for this external location of the testes is that the production of sperm is more efficient at temperatures lower than body temperature. Attached to each testicle is the epididymis, where sperm undergo maturation; during ejaculation they are propelled through the vas deferens and then out of the urethra.

Various concerns with the testicles and the scrotum involve physical changes, which are the result of anatomical defects. For example, if abdominal contents were allowed to pass into the scrotum, then this would be called an inguinal hernia. This presents as a prominent bulge in the groin or the scrotal region, especially upon straining or coughing. Manipulation of this bulge with your hand should easily pass the contents back into the abdomen; however, if the contents become stuck, then this needs to be addressed immediately. When a hernia is trapped, it can become strangulated, and then the blood supply is cut off. This can be excruciatingly painful and very dangerous because it can lead to gangrene. If a bulge develops in your scrotum or along the line that separates your abdomen from your lower extremity, seek medical attention.

Other causes of scrotal fullness can be attributed to a hydrocele, which is a collection of fluid. Most men let this painless accumulation go without consulting a doctor unless the heaviness or discomfort becomes unbearable. Causes include infection of the testicles or epididymis, trauma, or tumor. Ultrasound will confirm the presence of a hydrocele and treatment involves addressing the underlying cause.

In older men, medical problems associated with heart and liver disease can result in abnormal fluid collection in the lower extremities and the groin called edema. A failing heart or liver is incapable of processing normal volumes of blood. Overloading the heart or liver can result in accumulation of fluid in the legs and the scrotum. Treatment involves strict adherence to medical therapy. Often patients are treated with diuretics to alleviate excess volume, and patients are encouraged to facilitate the flow of fluid by keeping their feet up in the reclining position.

Spermatoceles are another painless condition that affects the scrotum. These are cysts that develop in the epididymis and that are filled with fluid containing dead sperm. Spermatoceles are the result of blocked sperm drainage. They are considered benign but can become quite discomforting if they get large enough. Patients usually present with small palpable round lesions along the epididymis. Diagnosis is made by ultrasound and treatment typically involves observation. Surgery is usually reserved for painful cysts.

Varicoceles are the result of defects in the valves or compression of the veins that drain the testicles. A swollen and enlarged collection of tortuous veins can appear. Often described as a "bag of worms," these are highly displeasing to most men due to the usual symptoms of scrotal swelling and testicular pain. Varicoceles commonly occur on the left side of the body and are strongly associated with infertility. These are a result of compromised blood flow to the testicle, which begins to shrink in size. Diagnosis is made by physical exam and confirmed with ultrasound. Scrotal support with a jock strap is usually the first line of therapy. Surgical intervention is reserved to reverse infertility, improve cosmetic appearance, and to reduce the size of an enlarged varicocele.

Infection of the scrotum that pertains to the testicles is called orchitis. If it affects the epididymis, then this is known as epididymitis. Both result in painful swelling of the affected area and can contribute to fluid collection, or a hydrocele. Men typically present with fever, swelling, and intense pain. Causes of orchitis can be either viral or bacterial. Most cases of viral orchitis are due to the mumps. Bacterial orchitis rarely occurs without an associated epididymitis. In sexually active men aged twenty to thirty-five, causes of orchitis and epididymitis are most often the result of sexually transmitted diseases, particularly gonorrhea or chlamydia.

Torsion of the testicles is probably the most dire situation that can affect the testicles. It usually appears in younger men as sudden intense pain in the scrotum after playing sports. It involves the actual twisting of the spermatic cord, which contains the blood supply to the testicle. Other causes include trauma or rough manipulation during sex. With torsion, men experience intense one-sided pain. Prompt diagnosis and treatment is necessary in order to salvage the testicle.

Blue balls is a slang term that you may have heard about in high school. When a male becomes sexually aroused, the arteries carrying blood to the genitalia engorge, while the veins carrying blood away from the genital area constrict. This volume overload of blood contributes to a penile erection, and likewise, the testicles become swollen. During this process of "vasocongestion" the testicles can increase in size by 25 to 50 percent. After you achieve orgasm, the arteries and veins return to their normal size. The volume of blood in the genitals becomes reduced and the penis and testes revert back to their original size. If ejaculation does not occur, there may be a lingering sensation of heaviness combined with discomfort coming from the testicles due to persistent "vasocongestion." This unpleasant feeling is what is referred to as blue balls, partly due to the bluish discoloration that appears when the testicles engorge with blood. Even if ejaculation is not achieved, the pain will eventually subside, but it can take up to an hour.

The testicular self-exam is an important function for all men and is as valuable to men as a self-exam of breasts is to women. In the shower, gently massage the skin of the scrotum. It should feel smooth and loose. Be sure to note any inconsistencies or irregularities. When you exam your testicles, focus on one at a time. Each should feel smooth and firm, like a large olive or small egg. Some men have naturally large testicles. Notice any nodules, bumps, or discrepancies between the two. Testicular cancer often affects men aged twenty to thirty-five. The cause of testicular cancer is unknown; however, most cases are curable if diagnosed early. Treatment depends on the type and stage of testicular cancer. Removal of the testicle is imperative, although the role of radiation or chemotherapy depends on the stage. Regular testicular self-examinations help detect dangerous growths early when the chance for successful treatment is the highest. So next time you take a shower, give yourself a good feel.

THE PROSTATE

The prostate is a muscular walnut-sized gland that sits in your pelvis beneath your bladder and in front of your rectum. The urethra runs from the bladder through the prostate carrying urine and seminal fluid to the opening of your penis. As part of the male reproductive system, its main job is to produce seminal fluid, which carries sperm. Sperm is produced by the testicles, which also make the male sex hormone testosterone. This then stimulates the growth and function of the prostate, especially throughout puberty. During orgasm, the prostate contracts in order to ejaculate seminal fluid through the urethra.

Conditions that affect the prostate more than likely relate to an infectious process or an anatomical defect. For the most part, prostate problems present similarly, with pain felt deep in the pelvis and difficulty in voiding. When these symptoms arise, most patients immediately become concerned about prostate cancer. This is an appropriate response, especially in the older population and those men with a family history, but this section will outline some of the more common conditions that affect gay men.

Prostatitis is the term for any inflammation of the prostate. It describes a variety of symptoms, including a frequent or urgent need to urinate combined with pain or burning upon voiding. Often accompanied by pelvic, groin, or low back pain, prostatitis affects nearly fifty percent of all men at some point in their lives. Characterized by several different forms, the four most common include acute and chronic bacteria prostatitis, nonbacterial prostatitis, and prostatodynia. In the United States over one million men will be treated annually for prostatitis, with chronic bacterial and nonbacterial being the majority of the cases. The most severe form is acute bacterial; it is the least common form yet makes up a large number of the cases that present to the emergency room.

Bacterial prostatitis is contracted when an organism makes its way up the urethra and infects the prostate. Acute prostatitis affects younger men and is often associated with sexually transmitted bacteria like gonorrhea and chlamydia. In older men, the most common causes include *Escherichia coli* (*E. coli*), *enterobacter, serratia,* and *pseudomonas.*

Since the rectum is a great home of bacteria, especially *E. coli*, barebacking (engaging in condomless anal sex) can expose your urethra to these organisms that can work their way up to your prostate. In addition to always using condoms, remember to void after ejaculation in order to prevent bacteria from settling in your urethra.

Some men who enjoy sticking objects in their urethras, such as catheters and metal rods called "sounds," need to be especially careful. Sterilize all your toys, especially after use, and never use saliva as a lubricant. The mouth harbors germs that can be hazardous to your urethra and prostate. Also make sure you do not insert anything in your urethra after it has been in your rectum or your mouth. Once again, remember to urinate after playtime.

The acute form of bacterial prostatitis usually presents with fever, chills, pain, and frequent urination. On the other hand, chronic prostatitis tends to develop more slowly and symptoms are usually not as severe. Treatment for both consists of a course of antibiotics typically for two weeks for the acute form and up to twelve weeks for the chronic type.

Men with nonbacterial prostatitis have signs of prostatic inflammation but no evidence of a bacterial infection. This type of prostatitis has been thought to be associated with heavy lifting, occupations like truck driving, jogging, bicycle riding, and receptive anal sex. Men who have similar complaints of pain but no evidence of inflammation likely have the fourth form of prostatitis, called *prostatodynia.* In this case a psychological component may be present.

Tips on prostate care include drinking plenty of water, limiting alcohol consumption, and using a "split" bicycle seat for those avid cyclists. Also avoid backup of fluid into the prostate by urinating regularly and having routine orgasms.

One of the most common conditions associated with the prostate is benign prostatic hyperplasia, or BPH. This commonly affects more than 50 percent of men over the age of sixty and nearly 90 percent of men aged seventy. The exact cause is not known but involves changes in the prostate induced by hormones, especially testosterone, which cause the prostate to enlarge. As the prostate grows, it begins to compress the urethra, which runs through it. This can disrupt the flow of urine. Men with BPH often complain of *frequency*, or an excessive sensation to void, especially at night. Men with frequency actually void very little. Often a man suffering from BPH will stand at a urinal for some time waiting for the flow of urine to begin. This is called *hesitancy*. Some men find that it takes a while to initiate urination and that they only can void small amounts. If urine backs up in the bladder as a result of an inability to void, this can result in a urinary tract infection or kidney stones. As part of the initial assessment and exam for all males aged forty and older, expect your doctor to query you on how often you get up at night to go to the bathroom. If the answer is two or more, you need to be worked up for BPH. Obviously if you drink a substantial amount after eight p.m., then it's wise to avoid doing so for a trial period to see if this corrects the problem.

A diagnosis of BPH is made by a review of a patient's symptoms in combination with a digital rectal exam. An enlarged prostate will feel firm, smooth, and rubbery in consistency. The PSA is elevated in less then 10 percent of the cases unless cancer is also present. Ultrasound will reveal an enlarged prostate; however, it is not essential in making the diagnosis. Men without symptoms usually require no treatment, while those with mild symptoms suggestive of urinary obstruction can benefit from medical therapy. Alpha bockers (Hytrin, Uroxatral, Cardura, and Flomax) [OU91] relax the smooth muscle cells of the prostate and bladder to increase the flow of urine. 5-alpha reductase inhibitors, such as Proscar (finasteride) or Avodart (dutasteride) can reverse the effects of the male hormones responsible for prostate growth and can decrease the average size of the prostate by up to 25 percent. Men who present with enlarged prostates and bothersome symptoms may benefit from combination therapy with both a 5-alpha reductase and an alpha blocker. Patients with severe or progressive symptoms despite medical therapy may require surgical intervention, called a transurethral resection of the prostate, or TURP. According to guidelines published by the American Urological Association, all men should be screened for enlarged prostates by age fifty.

THE ANUS

In order to discuss the anus it is important as gay men that we recognize it as both a functional and genital organ. To begin you must understand the anatomy. Simply put, the anus is the termination of the colon. The surface is covered in a thick skin called the anal epithelium and is supplied with a rich sensory nerve network. Passing beyond the anal verge about 1.5 cm is the dentate line. This acts as the border between the anus and the rectum. The surface of the rectum is frail and bleeds easily because it is covered by a delicate mucous membrane. Here there are no sensory nerves so diseases and conditions that develop in the rectum usually do not register as pain. For 12 cm the rectum passes through the pelvis up to the sigmoid region where it enters the abdomen and continues on as the colon. The rectal ampulla, located in the pelvis, is a storage space for feces. Upon defecation, stool is expelled through the anus.

There are numerous conditions beyond cancer of the colon and the anus that affect gay men. Understanding these conditions is vital because they can be closely associated with anal intercourse. The most common anorectal problem is hemorrhoids. These are protrusions of veins that normally line the rectum and the anus. Due to excessive straining, these veins protrude and can develop clots. Constipation and bearing down during receptive anal intercourse are common causes of hemorrhoids, and most patients complain of pain, especially while sitting down. Patients begin to suspect a problem when they defecate and notice blood on the toilet paper.

Hemorrhoids are divided into two categories. Internal hemorrhoids refer to the veins inside the rectum, and external hemorrhoids are associated with protrusions on the external surface of the anus. Diagnosis is made by direct visualization of the hemorrhoid or upon palpation during a digital rectal exam. Treatment involves addressing the underlying cause. In cases of constipation, stool softeners are recommended. Most cases of hemorrhoids respond to sitting in a tub of warm water (sitz bath) and applying a mild anti-inflammatory cream, like Preparation H, to the affected area. Normally, the protrusions resolve with these measures but complications can occur.

Cases of clot formation are referred to as thrombosed hemorrhoids. Treatment for these very painful variants requires removal of the clot by carefully incising the hemorrhoid with a scalpel and then manually expressing the contents. Once the clot has been evacuated, the pain resolves almost immediately. Further treatment with sitz baths and anti-inflammatory creams is recommended after removal of the clot.

The severity of the internal hemorrhoid dictates treatment. Over-the-counter anti-inflammatory suppositories reduce the swelling, along with stool softeners and sitz baths. In severe or recurrent cases, patients are referred to a gastroenterologist or a colorectal surgeon. Complex situations require visualization with the aid of a sigmoidoscope or an anoscope. Under direct visualization the internal hemorrhoids can be treated with rubber-band ligation, which is effective in almost 90 percent of the cases. Other modes of treatment involve cryotherapy, or freezing hemorrhoids, as well as electrodessication, or burning them off. Beyond that, if the hemorrhoids are too large or too many, surgeons recommend a hemorrhoidectomy with a sphincterotomy. This involves excising the entire hemorrhoid and then reapproximating the rectum with sutures. The procedure is done as a same-day surgery, but the recovery is painful.

Anal fissures are cracks or tears in the anal canal. Friction produces tears in the rectal mucosa, and as a result, pain leads to involuntary tightening of the internal anal sphincter. Fissures, like hemorrhoids, respond to stool softeners and sitz baths. Some, however, are the result of viral infections like herpes or sexually transmitted bacteria like gonorrhea. Both require medical therapy. Gay men commonly present with anal fissures especially after prolonged receptive anal sex. On exam a small tear is noted along the anus. Usually the fissure will resolve without further aggravating the area. Continued anal sex will disrupt the fissure and complicate the healing process. Nonhealing fissures should be reported to your doctor. Unfortunately, even if you refrain from anal sex, you still have to defecate, and this can make fissures worse. So what do you do? There are topical medications, like steroid creams, that can relieve discomfort and speed up recovery. Doctors have used topical nitroglycerin and botulinum toxin to relax the internal sphincter in order to expedite healing. Surgery is reserved for medical treatment failures and involves incising the sphincter to relieve pressure and to allow healing.

Anal fissures can also be the result of an underlying sexually transmitted disease. Common causes include herpes, syphilis, chlamydia, chancroid, and lymphogranuloma venereum. The presence of one STD at the site of an ulceration does not exclude another infection in the same lesion. There are reports of two or more pathogens detected in up to 20 percent of genital ulcers. The two most common are herpes simplex and syphilis.

A peri-rectal abscess is a collection of pus that develops in the rectal mucosa due to obstruction of the anal glands by a piece of stool, which can lead to a bacterial infection. Often, gay men shave the area around their anus and ingrown hairs can become infected. This produces a throbbing sensation on the inside of the rectum as the abscess develops. Over time it will increase in size if left untreated and begin to drain pus. In some cases the abscess will burrow into the skin and cause a track that opens up in the lower rectum. This is called a *fistula*. Patients typically present with a variety of complaints that include fever, rectal pain or pressure, a throbbing sensation, and discharge. Doctors usually make the diagnosis by examination alone, but in some advanced cases a CT scan may be required to visualize the extent of the

Dr. Frank's Tips on Healthy Bowel Movements

Most people at some point in their life will experience constipation. If you develop difficulty with passing your bowel movements or if you note a change in the caliber of your stool, then you should follow these tips:

1. Increase the amount of fiber in your diet by including whole grains, green leafy vegetables, fruits, and nuts (especially almonds).
2. Drink plenty of water. This will soften the stool.
3. Avoid caffeine.
4. Exercise regularly to promote colonic function.
5. Over-the-counter products such as Metamucil work to promote regular bowel movements, but if constipation persists, consult your doctor.

Change in bowel habits especially in older men can be a warning sign of something more ominous, like cancer. Don't be paranoid, but stay in tune with your body's performance. Having irregular bowel movements or constipation should always alert you to reexamine your diet and your lifestyle. If these symptoms persist beyond the ordinary measures to alleviate such a condition then consult your doctor.

IN 1996, I went to my first Black Party, an annual leather circuit party held at New York City's Roseland Ballroom. In addition to the thousands of sexy men dressed in leather, there were live sex shows taking place on a stage in the back of the hall. One show in particular left an indelible impression upon me. It involved a man dressed in a leather harness who sat atop a platform center stage. Using several dildos of increasing size, he began to display his talent of unhinged facial expression in light of anal penetration. With each new, larger dildo, the crowd roared violently and clenched their buttocks involuntarily. But just when I thought I had seen enough, this gentleman stood up and squatted on a police cone. It was an arresting visual to behold and one that haunts me to this day. Had I been this performer's doctor, I would have advised him on the future complication he would be facing with fecal incontinence. Although the anal sphincter is a tight muscular band, there is just so much it can withstand. Eventually, the muscles will lax and lose their tonicity if forced beyond a point for prolonged periods of time.

If I were his doctor, I would have instructed him that if he was to continue performing, he would need to practice Kegel exercises. Dr. Arnold Kegel, a gynecologist, described a technique known as Kegel exercises in order to strengthen the pubococcygeus muscle in women. Initially designed to help with urinary incontinence, it was later found that strengthening the pubococcygeus muscle also promoted increased sexual sensitivity and responsiveness in both women and men.

The way it works is simple. The pubococcygeus is a muscular sling that lines the floor of the pelvis. It extends from the pubic bone all the way to the coccyx above your anus. Contracting this muscle is done in two ways: The first involves taking a deep breath while you contract your muscles in order to clench your anus. Then while exhaling slowly, release the contraction. The other way involves short rhythmic contractions linked with breathing 20 or so times, then resting. Kegel exercises can be done anywhere, and with practice they can improve erections, intensify orgasms, and help to control rectal tension during anal penetration. Some literature suggests practicing while urinating in order to hold the flow of urine. This is not recommended because it can lead to urinary retention and subsequent infections.

abscess. Incision and drainage of the abscess may be warranted, but often oral antibiotics are sufficient in early cases. Complicated fistulas require surgical drainage in an operating room under anesthesia. Aftercare involves keeping the area clean and dry, soaking in warm water, and avoiding anal sex until fully healed.

Any major change in bowel habits can be an indication of an underlying condition. Constipation, like diarrhea, should alert you that something is wrong with your body. Defined as difficulty passing a bowel movement or less than three bowel movements in a week, constipation also includes passing dry, hard stools. Most people defecate regularly, but this is not the case for everyone. Regularity depends on what you eat. Normal cycles of defecation occur according to your body's metabolism. For the majority of people this means going on a regular basis and usually at the same time of day. Factors that contribute to constipation include low-fiber diets and dehydration. Sometimes the peristaltic action of the colon slows down due to increased tension or a sedentary lifestyle. These factors along with dietary changes can promote constipation. When the body is unable to pass feces regularly it builds up in the rectal ampulla and becomes hard. Passing a bowel movement once it has been allowed to accumulate can be painful and can contribute to hemorrhoids or fissures due to the straining in order to pass the stool. Even certain medications can result in constipation.

Common causes of constipation include some medications like pain killers, antidepressants, iron containing supplements, and some drugs used to control blood pressure. In addition, medical problems such as hypothyroidism and mechanical conditions like intestinal obstruction either due to a stricture or tumor can also lead to an inability to pass feces.

Dr. Frank's Tips on Anal Care

1. Check yourself in the mirror and get to know your anus.
2. Avoid constipation with a high-fiber diet and plenty of water.
3. Sit in a warm bath—this relaxes the muscles of the anus and rectum.
4. Remember that lubrication and condoms reduce the chance of damaging the anus and minimize the risk of transmitting disease.
5. Wash your anus before and after anal sex to reduce the amount of bacteria that can be spread.
6. Overuse of enemas can destroy the normal, healthy balance of bacteria in the lower intestine.
7. Pain or bleeding is a warning sign that should be looked into by your doctor.

Fecal incontinence is the loss of voluntary bowel control that is associated with a laxity of the muscles of the anal sphincter, often with nerve damage. Patients with incontinence are typically older and suffer from chronic disease states such as diabetes or Alzheimer's disease. Other causes are related to seizure disorders and stroke. Trauma to the muscular walls of the rectum can also result in incontinence. A common myth concerning gay men is that they develop fecal incontinence after prolonged receptive anal sex. The fact is that other circumstances that involve sex play with toys and fisting can be more damaging than penetrative anal sex with a penis.

Finally, anal itching is commonly associated with infections such as pinworms, condylomata, or candida, but it can also be related to skin disorders such as contact dermatitis and psoriasis. In rare cases, unknown causes can develop into idiopathic pruritus ani which is more common in men. Anal itching is usually self-limiting and can be treated with topical creams. Underlying infections need to be treated with the appropriate antibiotics.

CHAPTER 6

Gay Sex

GAY LIFE in the 1970s was a completely different world than now. My first introduction to gay existence involves the memory of my family driving through the West Village on our way to Little Italy. As we passed the piers along the West Side Highway during the hot summer months, scores of young men in tank tops and cut-off jeans blanketed the streets. "What a shame," remarked my older sister. "They're all so gorgeous." Even at the tender age of seven, I understood what she meant.

Four years later, I was invited to spend the weekend with a fellow schoolmate, Michael, at his uncle's apartment off Bank Street, in the West Village. Not so obvious to me at the time, his uncle was clearly gay, with his thick handlebar mustache, tight blue jeans, and the ever-present handkerchief stuffed in his back pocket. Later I learned that he was also a bartender at the legendary Ramrod Bar, which was immortalized after a tragic incident when a man opened fire on the patrons in 1980.

That weekend I discovered a fascinating world. Following Michael's uncle around the city, I viewed with great curiosity the way he communicated with other men. His subtle glances and stares conveyed a language that continues to this day among gay men. Often the purpose of this silent communication is to reveal our sexuality to one another and perhaps to express our interest.

In 1991, while visiting friends on Fire Island, I met an interesting couple on the ferry. They were celebrating their twenty-fifth anniversary together. Intrigued with this idea of communication, I asked them about gay life during the early years of their relationship. Had their methods of relating to one another changed significantly over the years? Interestingly, their answers were split. "Definitely," said William. "It was all about the unspoken word back then. We hinted with prolonged looks and subtle gestures. Now everything is out in the open."

His partner disagreed. "You're delusional," said David. "I remember wearing a bandana in my back pocket and cruising men in broad daylight while walking through the Meat Rack."

This reference to bandanas reminded me of Al Pacino's controversial movie *Cruising*, in which, among other things, the gay hanky code was introduced to mainstream America. Incidentally, the controversy over this movie became the driving force for every young homosexual to catch a glimpse of a side of gay life that had never been seen before. Its depiction of leather bars, drugs, and open sexual displays painted a dark view of gay life and left an indelible mark on how Americans perceive homosexuality.

Although the hanky code is considered antiquated by most gay men today, its significance in gay culture remains. It is symbolic of the way oppression forced gays to silently communicate without the threat of persecution. At its basic level, the placement of the bandana signified sexual preference with the left indicating that you preferred to "top" and the right indicating that you were looking to "bottom." Versatile gays had the option of tying their hanky to the rear center belt loop. Color corresponds to specific sex acts, and even the fabric of the hanky—lace, satin, corduroy, gingham, velvet—lends its own twist on the code. For a more detailed description, look up "gay hanky codes" on the Internet. On the next page is a list of some of the more common codes.

So much of what gay men know about sex is learned through watching pornographic movies, listening to friends, and ultimately through their experiences. Sexual freedom between two men found its heyday in the 1970s along with the sexual revolution that began in the 1960s; however, it was quickly squashed with the outbreak of HIV. In the early 1980s, HIV began to infect gay men and was first described as a gay cancer. Soon the epidemic took its toll as gay men began to die in record numbers. Places like sex clubs and bathhouses, which were once private sanctuaries for gay men to engage in anonymous sex, were being shut down due to the increased spread of HIV and other sexually transmitted diseases.

As gay men emerged from this epidemic, the use of condoms became a routine practice for gay men. Still, there is concern with how gay men perceive themselves sexually. There is a tendency for some to view sex as shameful and profane, and it is this aspect that leads to trouble. That is why it is imperative for all gay men to learn the fundamental aspects of gay sex.

Gay hanky codes

COLOR	LEFT	RIGHT
BLACK	HEAVY SM TOP	HEAVY SM BOTTOM
GRAY	BONDAGE TOP	LIKES TO BE TIED UP
BLUE, LIGHT	WANTS ORAL SEX	GIVES ORAL SEX
BLUE, NAVY	ANAL INTER-COURSE TOP	BOTTOM
RED	FISTING TOP	FISTING BOTTOM
PINK, LIGHT	SEX TOYS TOP	SEX TOYS BOTTOM
PINK, DARK	NIPPLE TORTURER	NIPPLE TORTUREE
MAGENTA	SUCK MY PITS	ARMPIT FREAK
LAVENDER	LIKES DRAG QUEENS	DRAG QUEEN
YELLOW	WATER SPORTS PISSER	WATER SPORTS PISSEE
GOLD	TWO LOOKING FOR ONE	ONE LOOKING FOR TWO
ORANGE	ANYTHING ANYTIME	JUST CRUISING
CORAL	SUCK MY TOES	SUCKS TOES
FUSCHIA	SPANKER	SPANKEE
GREEN, HUNTER	DADDY	BOY
OLIVE DRAB	MILITARY TOP	MILITARY BOTTOM

KISSING 101

In discussing sexual activity with patients and friends, it is a widely accepted fact that "the kiss" is the first intimate contact that connects two people. For some it is even the "deal breaker." The reason being that if you cannot kiss well together, then how compatible are you going to be sexually?

COLOR	LEFT	RIGHT
BEIGE	RIMMER	RIMMEE
BROWN LACE	UNCUT	LIKES UNCUT
BROWN SATIN	CUT	LIKES CUT
CHARCOAL	LATEX FETISH TOP	LATEX FETISH BOTTOM
GRAY FLANNEL	OWNS A SUIT	LIKES MEN IN SUITS
BLACK WITH WHITE CHECK	SAFE SEX TOP	SAFE SEX BOTTOM
RED WITH WHITE STRIPE	SHAVER	SHAVEE
RED WITH BLACK STRIPE	FURRY BEAR	LIKES BEARS
WHITE LACE	LIKES WHITE BOTTOMS	LIKES WHITE TOPS
BLACK WITH WHITE STRIPE	LIKES BLACK BOTTOMS	LIKES BLACK TOPS
BROWN WITH WHITE STRIPE	LIKES LATINO BOTTOMS	LIKES LATINO TOPS
PAISLEY	WEARS BOXER SHORTS	LIKES BOXER SHORTS
GOLD LAMÉ	LIKES MUSCLE-BOY BOTTOMS	LIKES MUSCLE-BOY TOPS
TAN	SMOKES CIGARS	LIKES CIGARS
TEDDY BEAR	CUDDLER	CUDDLEE

"Making out," or kissing with frottage, is a safe and fun way for new and old couples to connect. Kissing is great foreplay and acts to stimulate the erogenous zones. This can be particularly exciting if your partner has a sensitive neck and ears. Light, gentle kissing along the nape of the neck and up to the earlobe drives some men crazy. The trick is to experiment. Not everyone enjoys having breathy lips in their ear, but they might enjoy having you kiss their nipples and chest. Also the flanks, which are on either side of the abdominal muscles, are highly sensitive.

So what if you and your partner do not have a good kissing connection? Is this really the deal breaker? For some it is, but don't give up so easily. Sometimes all it takes is a little instruction and encouragement. New couples are especially nervous and early kissing encounters can be tense with rigid mouths or a jabbing tongue. Try to get your partner to relax and tell him what you like. Whatever you do, don't be rude, and if your partner criticizes your kissing, try to listen and not get insulted.

The risk of contracting disease from a kiss is variable. Some infections, especially herpes and mononucleosis, are easily transmitted by kissing. There are even reports of contracting syphilis and hepatitis B from deep, passionate kissing. In situations where you have open sores or bleeding gums, be particularly careful, since these areas act as portals for infection. HIV is not transmitted through kissing, although there is debate about one case report between a man and a woman.

MASTURBATION

In the movie *American Pie*, a young man masturbates with the aid of an apple pie. When he is discovered by his horrified parents, the result is a hilarious observation of how we as Americans view masturbation. As the viewers, we identify with the boy's humiliation because we have been taught that self-gratification is shameful and obscene. Parents, religions, and government agencies have been warning children against the perils of masturbation for centuries. Boys especially have been frightened into thinking that masturbation will lead to blindness, hairy palms, or worse, despite the lack of evidence to support these claims. Up until 1968, masturbation was listed as a mental disorder in the American Psychiatric Association's *Diagnostic and Statistical Manual.* Regardless, research by Alfred Kinsey showed that nearly all men masturbate at some point in their lives, and it should be considered a normal precursor to sexual relations.

Despite the threats, masturbation remains a rite of passage for young men. This act of self-discovery begins after puberty and for many boys comes completely by accident. To grab your penis with your hand and stroke it to the point where it becomes engorged to its full size and then progressing to the point of climax is an exhilarating revelation for young men.

A healthier attitude toward masturbation would see it as a natural progression through normal psychosocial development. Imagine the boy who learns to explore his body as someone who is curious and passionate. Devoid of guilt and shame, he grows up with an attitude toward sex that is less rigid and more sensual. Think about it: For most men forty and older, masturbation was a taboo subject. But the fact remains that many adult men claim that masturbation eases their depression and coaxes them into sleep.

As part of the sex act, mutual masturbation is the safest form of sex there is. Manually stimulating your partner's genitals offers tactile stimulation without the risk of STDs or HIV transmission. Self-masturbation in front of your partner can also be a very erotic experience. Show him how it is done and let him know what excites you. Masturbation completed to orgasm can be a gratifying encounter in and of itself. Long-term couples should utilize masturbation before proceeding to oral and anal sex if that is the inclination. The important thing to realize is that intimacy and sensuality play a role in good sex.

Perhaps if most gay men took slower steps toward intercourse we might not need so much Viagra. It is also incorrect to assume that once a man enters into a relationship he will abandon masturbation. Self-stimulation serves an adaptive purpose when the other member is unavailable or ill. Masturbation in these cases combines pleasure with tension release. For other men, despite having regular sexual relations with a partner, the experience of masturbation still provides an alternative that can be considered habitual or a way to stroke one's ego. Many men even in relationships continue to masturbate because it is an easy way to get off. For newer couples especially, kissing with massage and masturbation can be a wonderful holding pattern as you get to know each other better.

In addition to traditional penile masturbation, gay men also utilize the anus as a genital organ. Masturbation with anal manipulation is relatively common on its own or during penile masturbation. Receptive men enjoy a well-lubricated finger or their partner's tongue to stimulate this highly sensitive area. Anal digitation is also highly recommended as a precursor to anal intercourse in order to relax the muscles of the external anal sphincter. For good results, have your partner lie on his back, and using a well-lubricated gloved finger, insert it just beyond the anal verge. Begin slowly by working your finger in and out at first. For maximum pleasure advance your finger beyond the verge until you come upon a smooth ovoid mound. This is the prostate. Gently massage the prostate with your digit, pressing downward, for maximum pleasure. Prostatic massage can be very stimulating and can even provoke orgasm in some men. Use caution and check in with your partner. Conversely, if you are being penetrated and pain develops, stop all activity at once. Then see my tips on anal self-care. If pain or prolonged bleeding ensues, consult your doctor.

ORAL SEX

Oral sex refers to stimulating your partner's genitals by using your mouth or tongue. Often considered taboo in many cultures, oral sex dates as far back as the *Kama Sutra* and ancient Rome. Considered a sin by many religions because it does not support procreation, those who insisted upon engaging in such acts were often chastised and considered undesirable. Fellatio, or what is commonly known as a blow job, is the act of sucking and exerting friction on your partner's penis using your mouth. It has been suggested that the term is derived from the orgasm in which the recipient "blows" his load like a volcano.

Techniques vary from one person to the next, with some simultaneously caressing the shaft of the penis with their hand while rhythmically sucking their partner's penis. Alternately, some men find it pleasurable if you also lick the shaft of their penis and testicles intermittently. Throughout the experience your partner may emit a small amount of ejaculatory fluid, called pre-cum, which is not semen, although it can contain some sperm. Some men can orgasm by receiving fellatio, while others cannot. Depending on the person, an orgasm will produce a significant amount of semen. This fluid can transmit infections, especially gonorrhea, chlamydia, herpes, and syphilis. Although there is still debate about the risk of HIV transmitted through oral sex, most clinicians agree that swallowing ejaculation increases your susceptibility. One study quoted the statistic 1 in 10,000. Professional consensus dictates that swallowing ejaculation is not a good idea unless you are in a long-term monogamous relationship. Ultimately the choice is yours. If you're concerned about HIV or other sexually transmitted diseases then you should insist that your partner wear a condom while you perform oral sex. This would seem unreasonable to many; however, if you are having multiple anonymous sex partners then you increase your likelihood of infection by not using condoms. Accidents do happen, however, and if the condom breaks or your sex partner ejaculates in your mouth, spit the ejaculate out at once and rinse your mouth with salt water or gargle with Listerine. This is not 100 percent effective, but it's better than doing nothing at all. In addition to STDs, there are cases of pharyngitis, or infections of the throat, caused by trauma to the delicate pharyngeal tissue by a penis. When the head of the penis repeatedly hits the back of the throat, it can seed the tissue with bacteria. This is another good reason to gargle after performing oral sex.

The chemical components of ejaculatory fluid are primarily made up of water, with some fructose, salt, and protein. The salt content contributes to its alkalinic properties, and that is why it tastes bitter. The myth that ejaculating on someone's face is good for their skin is false. Although it can be considered hot, do it because you enjoy it, not because someone has falsely convinced you that it is good for your skin.

Part of the problem with performing oral sex is that it can be an anxiety-provoking prospect for some men who fear they may trigger their gag reflex. Any contact with the backmost portion of your mouth can result in a violent wretch. Many men recall the trauma induced when their pediatrician attempted to depress their tongue with that awful wooden stick. Experts in the art of fellatio boast an ability to suppress their natural gag reflex. This is what is commonly referred to as "deep throating," after the famous pornographic film *Deep Throat*, in which the star, Linda Lovelace, made famous the act of taking an entire penis into her mouth by learning to suppress her gag reflex. This ability is a learned response and takes practice to achieve. A good way to begin is to lie down on your back with your head hanging off the bed so that your head is fully extended. This elongates the oral cavity so that when your partner introduces his penis into your mouth, the gag reflex will not be triggered so readily. Full suppression of the gag reflex will take more than one try, so do not get discouraged.

How well you perform fellatio does not depend exclusively on your technique but also on how your partner responds to what you are doing. Ask him what he likes and listen for cues like moaning or verbal commands. Some men enjoy grasping their partner's head while thrusting it up and down on their penis. This type of aggressive behavior needs to be negotiated so that it is pleasing to both members. I had a patient named Alex who complained that his partner used to force his penis into the back of his throat until his eyes watered and he nearly vomited. He said that his partner got a perverse thrill out of watching him choke. This type of domination during a sex act is not uncommon. Although there are some men who enjoy being overpowered in this way, you should be clear about it if you do not. The history of oral sex as a passive act dates back to ancient Rome when eunuchs were considered submissive because they only had their mouths to offer sexually. Today some men enjoy role-play with an even exchange of passive and dominant characteristics. The bottom line is that this has to be agreed upon beforehand by both members, and if you don't like being treated submissively, tell your partner.

The topic of oral sex also pertains to the act of

stimulating your partner's anus with your mouth and tongue, called aniligus, or rimming. Since the anus has a rich sensory network, it is very sensitive to the actions of the mouth and tongue. Some men who receive oral-anal stimulation find it very pleasurable. Often men find that having their anus manipulated in this way relaxes their sphincter muscles and prepares them for penile penetration. There are many men who thoroughly enjoy performing oral-anal sex, and the act of "eating out" their partner provides them with an overwhelming sense of satisfaction and stimulation.

Licking and sucking your partner's anus while separating his buttocks can be done through a number of positions. Common for some is having their partner lie on his back, bent over, or flat on his stomach. Aniligus, however, is not for everyone. Some men have told me that they are worried about the health risks associated with oral-anal sex, and it is true that some organisms—especially hepatitis A, intestinal parasites, and herpes—are commonly transmitted through this route. Also, performing fellatio after oral-anal contact can transmit bacteria into your partner's urethra, causing a urinary tract infection. Although oral-anal sex is considered unsafe behavior, its association with HIV transmission is difficult to predict. Theoretically, if there is blood in the stool or open cuts or sores on the anus, then HIV could be transmitted. It would be wise to look before you leap. A good tip is to check things out first, and if the area doesn't look or smell right, then avoid it.

ANAL SEX

Considered a taboo by many cultures and religions, anal sex is nevertheless a fairly common practice among both heterosexual and homosexual couples. Anal sex between men was a traditional practice in ancient Greece and medieval Japan as a way for older mentors to impart their wisdom to their younger students. This relationship was not considered homosexual but pederasty, as these young men submitted themselves to their elders in order to receive wisdom, knowledge, and masculinity.

Conversely, in the United States, we have such strong moral concerns over oral and anal sex, and up until recently sodomy laws were in effect in many states. The impact of this legislation was negative, and this is one of many reasons that anal sex is not discussed openly. Despite all the bad press, Americans still engage in anal sex. In Edward O. Laumann's landmark book, *The Social Organization of Sexuality: Sexual Practices in the United States*, he reported that of the more than three thousand people interviewed, about 20 percent of heterosexuals and 80 percent of homosexuals engaged in anal sex. In a sex survey conducted by the *Advocate* in 1994, roughly 40 percent of gay men enjoyed insertive anal sex, while 43 percent enjoyed receiving it. These statistics were substantial despite the AIDS epidemic, which peaked in the 1980s. The reports that transmission rates for HIV and STDs were higher in men who engaged in unprotected anal sex discouraged many from engaging in intercourse. As our knowledge of the virus grew, however, gay men resumed their sexual practices, changed forever by the reality of condoms.

Anal sex, by definition, is the stimulation of the anus through the use of the mouth, fingers, or the penis. Most, however, regard anal sex exclusively as intercourse with insertion of the penis into the anal orifice. For homosexuals, this involves designating one partner as the insertive (top) or the receptive (bottom.). Although some men stake claim to only one role, recent studies show that more and more couples admit to being versatile, with both members taking on receptive and insertive roles. In interviewing hundreds of gay couples in my practice, I found some interesting trends. Most long-term couples admit that they are versatile, but for the most part, the sexual roles are established early on. Incidentally, the sexual role does not coincide with the balance of power in the relationship. Much like heterosexual couples, the masculine partner is not necessarily the one that runs the household. We have all witnessed our share of mothers who have ruled the roost. Conflicts that arise when one member wishes to change his sexual role and the other is not in agreement are usually symbolic of a power struggle. This dispute is less likely to be about sex than about something else.

In looking at the sexual and social behavior of homosexuals from the past to the present, there have been major advances in how we view the recipient partner. For a long time, the bottom was considered passive, feminine, and submissive. Conversely, the top was seen as dominant, masculine, and authoritative. These sexual roles can be a source of conflict for some gay men, especially the bottom. Although some men embrace these gender assignments, the majority do not. The more modern approach is not to associate anal sex position as being either masculine or feminine, but simply as being gay. Much of the struggle of coming to grips with your bottomhood is learning to overcome these ridiculous labels. Embrace the pleasurable aspects of anal sex and try to avoid the pitfalls of these labels.

Anal intercourse embodies a physical as well as a psychological component. There are some men who enjoy being the passive receptive partner and readily take on this role. For those men there is no cause for concern. On the other hand, there is a subgroup of gay men who enjoy receptive anal sex yet do not see themselves as passive. These "power bottoms" have reclaimed their status with regard to their sexual needs while maintaining their masculinity. This wonderful example displays how gay men can take up their personal authority when they know what they want and not allow themselves to feel abnormal or less of a man because of it. On the contrary, there are extreme cases where men have such guilt attached to being gay that they live as gay men but inhabit a sexual closet. They are in a vicious cycle that involves secretly participating in receptive anal sex but then condemning it publicly, followed by punishing themselves for it afterward. These characteristics perpetuate their issues with internalized homophobia. Often the emptiness they feel inside is in response to a lack of self-esteem. Some gay men often get themselves into trouble with sex based on the very issue of self-hatred. Filling the void by engaging in unsafe sexual practices in turn will drive these men further toward despair, guilt, and into depression.

The predominant issue with anal sex involves the mechanics of the act itself. Most men are concerned with the typical worries like, pain, feces, and damage. To truly enjoy anal intercourse it is paramount that a man understand the anatomy and function of the anus and rectum. Only then, with such demystification, can you enjoy the pleasures that your anus can provide. Instructing gay men on how to enjoy anal sex involves a simple outline of the anatomy and rectum, which was reviewed previously in the chapter, "The Anatomy of Sex."

We all know that the natural function of the rectum and anus is to defecate. The rectal ampulla is a storage space for feces, and once a sufficient amount has been collected, it expands and stimulates the walls to contract, which gets interpreted as a reflexive response to bear down. In order to receive a penis into your rectum it is imperative that you learn to counteract this instinctual response. Much like the gag reflex, this takes practice. To begin, prepare the anus for intercourse by gentle stimulation with either a finger or your partner's tongue. Some men find that if they have their anus stimulated in these ways, they are able to relax mentally for intercourse. Unlike the vagina, the rectum does not produce its own lubrication; that is why it is vital that you use a sufficient amount to ease the discomfort. Utilizing a water-based lubricant will not only increase the pleasure but reduce the risk of acquiring or transmitting STDs. Avoid lubricants with strong scents or chemicals because they can irritate your anal mucosa. In addition, latex condoms should be used to reduce the risk of transmitting STDs and HIV. Do not use oil-based lubricants with latex condoms because oil can damage the latex.

Once you are ready to begin, the receptive partner should lie on his back. The insertive partner should ease the head of his penis into the anal orifice and then stop. At this point, the muscles of the external anal sphincter will contract involuntarily. The receptive partner should then take slow deep breaths because the muscles of the external sphincter will eventually begin to relax. Once the receptive partner is comfortable, the insertive partner should then introduce the shaft of his penis into the rectum and then stop again. This will activate the muscles of the internal anal sphincter to contract. Once again take slow deep breaths to relax these muscles. At this point, your partner should begin to slowly withdraw his penis and then rhythmically reintroduce it. The motion ultimately depends on your comfort. All beginners should remember that slow and steady wins the race.

There are numerous positions to try. For beginners it is highly recommended that you start out with the receptive partner on top; this way you have more control. Straddling your partner, position his penis with your hand toward your anal orifice. Upon exhalation, introduce the penis into your anus and slowly sit down. Allow yourself to relax while modulating your breath, and—ta-da!—contact! Once your partner is inside you, maintain this position for several deep breaths to make adjustments. Your comfort is necessary before you proceed. The repetitive movement of the penis in and out of the rectum will stimulate the prostate, and for some men this can be very exhilarating. Since the prostate contracts upon stimulation to produce an orgasm, simultaneous masturbation during receptive anal sex has been known to produce an increased orgasmic response. That's something to think about for all you hard-core tops who might never have had the inclination to try bottoming. During the sex act it is recommended that you check in with your partner to make sure that you are both in synch mentally. Don't be afraid to talk during sex. Experiment. Change positions. It's all good as long as both of you are on the same page.

MALE DOUCHING

No one likes a messy bottom, but quite frankly that's the reality of anal sex. Many gay patients are concerned about anal sex, and one of their biggest fears is the potential for embarrassment. Along with the fear of pain, this fear keeps many gay men from participating in anal intercourse. The rectal ampulla is the portion of the rectum that stores feces until defecation expels the contents. During anal sex the motion of the penis in and out of the rectum and anus promotes the urge to defecate. This can make the bottom feel very uncomfortable. Sometimes fecal material can be passed without the receptive partner's awareness. In such cases there is no need to make an issue of it. A good tip is to place a towel under the receptive partner in order to avoid contamination with fecal material and lubricant. After sex if you both notice that there has been an accident, simply remove the condom and clean yourself off with some soap and water. A good tip is to remove the condom from the base—by doing so any fecal material or body fluid will be contained inside the condom. Remember: The idea is not to make a big deal out of it. If during intercourse the receptive partner feels a strong urge to defecate, he should simply stop, excuse himself, and go to the bathroom.

Most gay men use enemas commonly purchased in drugstores, which use the active ingredients of sodium and phosphate, along with a powerful laxative to cleanse the bowel before engaging in receptive anal sex. Men find that using an enema relaxes them so that they are not preoccupied with passing feces during intercourse. The proper use of the enema is to relieve constipation or as a bowel cleansing for surgery. Used correctly, the enema can provide safe relief by inducing complete emptying of the left colon, usually within one to five minutes, without pain or spasm. These over-the-counter enemas, like the Fleet brand, come in a plastic bottle with a lubricated tip. If you need to clean yourself out quickly, use the enema as directed on the box. Bend over and insert the applicator into your anus and squeeze. Try to hold it in for at least one minute and then release the contents into the toilet. If you don't feel clean enough, fill the bottle with warm tap water and repeat the process. Reusable plastic devices, like bulb syringes for ear irrigation, can also be

Dr. Frank's Sex Tips

1. Always use a condom.
2. Urinate after orgasms.
3. Never share razors, toothbrushes, and enema equipment. Harmful blood-borne bacteria, especially hepatitis, can live on minute blood particles.
4. Gargle after sex with mouthwash or salt water.
5. Shower after sex whenever possible.
6. Always use condoms on sex toys, especially if they are to be shared.

bought in a drug store and do not contain a laxative ingredient. With these devices, use warm tap water.

Using more than one enema in twenty-four hours can be harmful. Listen! Enemas contain a powerful irritant that causes the release of stool. Prolonged use will cause the lining of the rectum to erode and slough off, which can lead to bleeding and rectal discharge. A good idea instead is to save the plastic device and use tap water to clean yourself out. It's less harmful on the rectum and does the job just as well. Overdosage or retention may lead to severe electrolyte disturbances, including high sodium, high phosphate, low calcium, and low potassium, as well as dehydration and low blood pressure. Treatment of electrolyte imbalance may require immediate medical intervention with appropriate electrolyte and fluid replacement.

Do not use laxative products when nausea, vomiting,

or abdominal pain is present unless directed by a physician. If you notice a sudden change in bowel habits that persists over a period of two weeks, consult a physician. Rectal bleeding or failure to have a bowel movement after the use of a laxative may indicate a serious condition. Discontinue use and consult a physician. Laxative products should not be used longer than one week unless directed by a physician.

Some gay men forego the use of store-bought enemas and use a device that attaches to their shower head in order to provide a constant flow of water higher into the rectum. Water pressure is a major concern, since high pressure can cause perforation of the colon. Also, remember to use warm to cool tap water and avoid hotter temperatures because the sensitive rectal mucosa can burn easily.

CHAPTER 7

Fetishes, Fisting, and Water Sports . . . Oh My!

SEXUAL EXPLORATION is a natural inclination for most people regardless of sexual orientation. Traditional methods for experimentation include trying out various sexual positions as well as venturing outside the bedroom to do so. Beyond mainstream sex is another world inhabited by people who take pleasure by indulging in the fetish lifestyle. Defined as an object or body part that brings about sexual arousal, a fetish can be any number of things. From feet to dildos, black socks to jock straps, these objects act to heighten the sexual response.

A true fetish involves sexual activity that is directed toward an object, like masturbating while sniffing a jock strap. For others, a fetish is merely a way to refresh their sexual relationship by incorporating the object into sexual intercourse, like having your partner penetrate you while wearing a jock strap. In either case, the fetish acts to provide an additional means for a heightened sexual response and hopefully does not replace human interaction. Usually, the attachment to a fetish begins by adolescence and persists throughout adulthood.

Leather is a highly popular fetish, especially in the gay community, with bars and clubs designed to cater to the leather crowd. Most gay men admit that they have found themselves in a leather bar at some point in their lives, and even though the majority do not subscribe to this lifestyle, there are elements associated with it that are sexually enticing. For one, leather is associated with S&M.

Sadomasochism, or S&M, is a term that unites two separate but related entities—sadism and masochism. The sadist is the one who likes to inflict pain and is a term derived from the Marquis de Sade, an eighteenth-century French author who wrote and enacted violent sexual acts. According to the *Diagnostic and Statistical Manual of Mental Disorders* (DSM), sadism is a defense against fears of castration in which the sadist inflicts on others what they fear will happen to them. Alternately, masochism is taken from the acts of Leopold von Sacher-Masoch, a nineteenth-century Austrian novelist whose characters derived sexual pleasure from being dominated. The DSM describes masochists as those with a preoccupation for sexual arousal obtained from being humiliated. Often the two terms are combined as sadomasochistic behavior, and describe a relationship that encompasses pain, domination, and submission, but not necessarily through sex. These themes resonate profoundly in the gay community where issues of persecution can lead some gay men to act out violent sexual acts against other men who enjoy the degradation.

Along with the themes of S&M is the strong association with the iconic dress code. Leather gear, like boots, chaps, and pants, as well as chains and harnesses make up the attire of the leather community. In some cases gay men have also appropriated elements of police uniforms and army fatigues as well as other military wear as they embody symbols of strength, power, and masculinity. In addition to the iconic clothing, there are also distinct types of grooming where gay men fashion themselves with beards, mustaches, and shaven heads.

For die-hard members, S&M personifies more then just a costume. It is a way of life and reflects the domination that is perpetuated in our everyday existence. Gay men who devote themselves to this world see it as a way to reverse the oppression that they are subjected to by their prejudiced heterosexual counterparts. Regardless of your own strength of conviction, S&M, leather bars, and the fetish lifestyle exist throughout the United States, and the scene is as serious as you want it to be. Essentially, it is a way for like-minded men to congregate.

For instance, the Folsom Street Fair in San Francisco is the nation's largest annual leather event celebrating the fetish lifestyle. Hundreds of thousands of men and women convene to take part by dressing in leather outfits. Held on the last Sunday in September, this daytime fair is one of the largest outdoor events in California.

Visitors come from all over the world dressed in kinky leather outfits or military uniforms while being entertained with music and various public acts of bondage. Likewise, the Black Party in New York City is another annual event that celebrates the leather lifestyle, but in contrast to the Folsom Street Fair, the atmosphere is darker and heavier. Originally started at the now-defunct club, the Saint, where marathon dance events were held, the Black Party was a celebration of the spring equinox. After the demise of the Saint, the event continues on at the Roseland Ballroom where organizers encourage attendees to dress "heavy." For some critics, these events celebrate a decadent lifestyle that glamorizes recreational drugs and unsafe sex.

SEX TOYS

According to neurologist and psychiatrist Sigmund Freud's psychosexual stages of development, a disruption during the anal stage, which typically occurs from two to three years of age, results in an inability to resolve conflicts, and this can result in anal-retentive behavior or anal-expulsive fixations.

> As the physical ability to control the sphincter matures, the child's attention shifts from the oral to the anal zone. This change provides further outlets for libidinal gratification (anal eroticism) and for the emerging aggressive drive (anal sadism). The concept of fixation kicks in here. When there is excessive gratification in this stage, it leads to the development of extremely generous, unorganized personalities. When gratification does not occur, the individual becomes extremely organized.

It is a childlike fixation for some adults to revert back to their anal stage of development in order to experiment with their bodies. Dr. Ruth Westheimer, a renowned sex therapist, radio personality, and author, openly discussed human sexual practices and often remarked about the use of inanimate objects for the sake of sexual exploration. From sex toys like dildos, vibrators, and butt plugs to even stranger cases involving Coke bottles, vegetables, and even fruit, men's preoccupation with the rectum and anus has been proven consistently.

Psychiatrists interviewed with regard to anal fixation were inconclusive about such behavior. Although most agree that it is a common practice for both homosexual and heterosexual people, there is disagreement concerning why some take pleasure in extreme forms of anal penetration using foreign objects. The main concern is that taken to extremes, anal play with sex toys can have untoward consequences, although when done properly, it can be extremely pleasurable.

To start, men who wish to explore this erogenous area should begin with a well-lubricated gloved finger. You or your partner should gently massage the anus until it relaxes and then proceed by inserting the finger into the rectum. This will give you the opportunity to get comfortable. In choosing a sex toy, it is best to start off small and work your way up. Most men begin with a dildo or butt plug. Be sure to pick one with a prominent base so that it is easier to manipulate and harder to loose contact with. Cover it with a condom before insertion in order to avoid contact with fecal material or other bodily fluids. This is especially important if these objects are to be shared with other partners. Before insertion get into a comfortable position—either on your side or on your

ONE COUPLE who had an extensive collection of sex toys purchased a device called the Magic Egg while vacationing in Montreal. This is a small ovoid-shaped object that gets implanted in the rectum. Older models are connected via wire to a remote control that provides variable degrees of vibration as well as modulations to expand and contract. They spent an entire Sunday afternoon watching television on the couch while one partner stimulated the other. A year later I saw them at a party, and as we chatted, one produced a small remote from his pocket. The magic egg was now wireless! In addition to the wireless feature, the new, improved Baby Egg provided seven degrees of vibration and was waterproof. The Internet is a great resource for anal electrostimulation devices. There are even dual electronic products that provide simultaneous stimulation to both the penis and the rectum.

back—so that you will be able to fully manipulate the object yourself.

As you introduce the device into the anal orifice, breathe deeply in order to relax the muscles of the external anal sphincter. Once you feel comfortable, advance

Dr. Frank's Tip on Sex Toys

1. All new dildos should be washed with soap and water before use and thoroughly dried to avoid fungal buildup.
2. To maintain the cleanliness of your dildo, remember to always use a condom before insertion and wash them thoroughly afterward with soap and water, especially for plastic and latex sex toys. Also apply some rubbing alcohol for sterility.
3. Silicone products resist extreme temperatures and a good idea is to throw them in the dishwasher and let it do all the work.
4. Also dispose of dildos after a sufficient period of time. A good rule is to change them every six months.

the object further into your rectum while maintaining deep breaths as it passes through the internal anal sphincter. Since the rectum curves as it passes through the pelvis, straighter, less malleable toys like vibrators may meet some resistance at this point. Objects should always slide in without too much force. Do not *push* anything into your rectum. If you are uncomfortable, try changing positions or using more lubricant while maintaining deep breathing.

With experience you will be able to read your own body's response. Pay close attention to warning signs like pain, irritation, and bleeding. Often men who force objects in too quickly develop an irritated feeling afterward. Cease any further activity and see tips on anal care. If symptoms persist, consult your doctor. In cases where objects become irretrievable, try not to panic. Anxiety will result in muscle spasms. One approach to recovering foreign objects requires squatting while bearing down in order to allow gravity and muscular contraction to help. If this does not work, seek medical attention immediately!

In Jack Morin's amazing book, *Anal Pleasure and Health,* he states, "Certain widely held attitudes toward rectal stimulation are so negative and confusing that they can easily block anyone's ability to enjoy it." For gay men who contend with internalized homophobia, the reaction to rectal stimulation is very strong. Morin writes, "For these men anal tension is a natural reaction against real desires they're having trouble accepting." In some cases it takes time for gay men to get over these irrational feelings, but for others it is a no win situation. Exploring anal gratification is not for everyone, and medical problems can arise when there is a lack of information. Healthy sexual exploration is normal, but it necessitates understanding the anatomy and function of the rectum and anus.

FISTING

The idea that for some men, sexual pleasure is achieved by the insertion of a hand into their rectum is very intriguing. Contrary to how it sounds, fisting actually involves inserting the fingers into the rectum so that the tip of the thumb touches the other fingers in the shape of a cone. Anal manipulation with fingers and then the whole hand is a unique experience and very different from having your bottom penetrated by a sex toy or penis. Regular fisting bottoms often start off with merely a finger inserted into the rectum while masturbating alone. These early steps help to facilitate anal penetration by teaching you to relax with breathing exercises while getting to know your body. Paired with a partner, bottoms work their way up to fisting by having their partner perform digital insertion and penile intercourse first.

Receptive men who would like to attempt getting fisted should proceed cautiously at first. Accommodating fingers, a hand, and perhaps a wrist requires a tremendous amount of trust, relaxation, and self-awareness. As always, use a latex glove and begin with a well-lubricated finger that is slowly introduced into the anus. Upon insertion, attempt using two fingers and work your way up by allowing time in between each additional insertion so that the receptive partner can adjust to the change in capacity. This will take time. Eventually, the insertive partner will get to a point where he can admit his fingers with the thumb touching the other digits in the shape of a cone. Men who have engaged in receptive fisting report intense and deeply satisfying sensations. The experience is a combination of mutual trust and emotional surrender. There are even couples who equate these intense encounters with a spiritual experience. The fact is that fisting requires time and dedication, and this is certainly not an activity to consider if you are looking for a quickie.

For S&M enthusiasts the pleasure gained from fisting is twofold. For the inserter it is an act of domination because the hand, unlike the penis, is a completely manipulative appendage. As for the receptive partner, the eroticism lies in the ability to surrender control and learn to relax.

THE FIRST TIME I encountered a patient with an irretrievable foreign object was on a quiet Friday night in the ER. A male nurse named Paul woke me up in the call room and handed me the chart with a Cheshire cat grin. Staring at the diagnosis, Paul had written, F.O. (foreign object) with a smiley face in the O.

"That's right, doll face," he said. "You're on."

Inside the GYN room, I found Robert, a thirty-five-year-old male, lying on the exam table huddled in the fetal position moaning quietly. He had inserted a dildo into his rectum four hours earlier and was unable to remove the object. After performing a rectal exam, I was able to palpate the tip of the base of this dildo. I instructed Paul to administer some sedation in order to relax the

Both participants need to be knowledgeable about the rectal anatomy. The lining of the rectum is fragile and prone to perforation or tears due to long nails, rings, and extensive play. Bleeding is another common consequence and needs to be addressed medically if it does not abate. In addition to always wearing latex gloves, the use of a thick

patient, and after fifteen minutes of prolonged steady traction, I was able to remove
it. As I fell back onto the floor with the dildo
on my lap, Paul exclaimed, "It's a boy!"

Other similar cases were not so easily
remedied. One of the more challenging involved a fifty-year-old male who inserted a
vibrator into his rectum. Like Robert, he
was also unable to retrieve it. Unfortunately,
he panicked, which resulted in muscle
spasms. Completely and utterly embarrassed
by what he had done, this gentleman waited
nearly five days before seeking medical
attention. By the time he presented to the
ER, he had developed a fever, along with
severe lower abdominal pain. This patient
was diagnosed with a perforation of the colon that resulted in sepsis, a blood infection.
He was taken to the operating room to remove the vibrator and repair the colon. He
survived but remained in the ICU for two
weeks.

water-based lubricant like J-Lube is recommended—and it
provides a slick surface. The bottom line is to use plenty
of lube to ensure safety and comfort.

Some fisting aficionados use Crisco or other oil-based
lubricants such as the commercially prepared Slam
Dunk or Boy Butter because they provide a slicker surface.

ONCE A TALL, LANKY MAN with a tattoo of a snake spiraling up his neck confided to me that he was a fisting top. This is something he enjoyed more than intercourse, he said. In fact, his exact words were, "I'm a fisting top, and I don't take amateurs." As a surgical resident, one of my many duties was to disempact elderly patients who developed chronic constipation. Dislodging rockhard fecal material with my hand in their rectum was no picnic, and it certainly was never erotic. As the snake-tattooed fisting pro described his talents, I laughed to myself thinking that the chore I had to endure for the sake of medicine was a task he relished with delight.

Oil-based lubricants are better at reducing friction; however, they are not recommended for use with latex products. Also during these intense sessions it is strongly discouraged to companion fisting in tandem with penile intercourse.

Aggressive fisting can result in cuts, abrasions, or tears in the skin of the rectum or the hand, which may result in the transmission of bacteria and infections like HIV. Change gloves routinely and wash your hands thoroughly. There are documented cases of skin infections or cellulitis of the hand, as well as synovitis, or inflammation of the fluid-filled tendon sheath, due to bacterial infection. Infections are common when there are breaks in the skin that can act as a portal to harmful bacteria. Look for signs like pain, swelling, and redness to alert you to a possible infection of the hand.

WATER SPORTS

Urolagnia, also known as urophilia, is sexual pleasure associated with the desire to urinate on your partner or to

AN INTERESTING take on the theme of water sports involves pleasure that is derived from having a partner ingest large amounts of fluid and then not being permitted to use the bathroom. One couple had a routine that involved going to their local leather bar and drinking beer all night. As the night progressed one was not allowed to use the restroom. This partner's growing sense of desperation was the driving force for the dominant partner's sexual arousal. The subordinate gained pleasure from the humiliation involved. At a certain point they would return home and the evening culminated with the subordinate voiding on the other partner as he masturbated on the floor of the shower.

be urinated upon. Commonly referred to as "golden showers," it can also be performed in conjunction with masturbation. Some men who partake in water sports also enjoy having their partner urinate in their mouths. Since urine is a sterile byproduct of blood that is filtered through the kidney, the risk for contracting infection is low unless urine is retained in the bladder for prolonged periods of time. Infected urine can be concentrated, appears darkly colored, and often tastes bitter. While HIV has been found in urine, it is not concentrated in an amount sufficient for transmission. In the S&M world, the subordinate partner enjoys being pissed on or taking his partner's urine into his mouth as a form of humiliation and pleasure.

Another form of urethral eroticism involves sexual stimulation by passing objects like metal rods into the urethra. In general, instrumentation of the urethral orifice is strongly discouraged for fear of a potential tear. Warning signs for such damage include bright red blood upon urination. This warrants immediate medical attention! Blood in the urethra has a tendency to clot and this will lead to urinary retention.

Included in water sports is enema play in which partners gain pleasure from receiving or giving an enema. The release of fluid is erotic for some men, and those who enjoy the exercise often have their favorite way to receive one. This includes using bulb syringes or appliances that attach to the shower. Regular tap water is recommended for this use. Avoid irritant laxatives and alcohol enemas. The risk for intoxication is very high and the absorption potential is fast. There are even reported deaths in some cases. Repetitive enemas with laxatives can also be harmful to the colon.

CHAPTER 8

Barebacking and HIV Post-Exposure Prophylaxis

BAREBACKING

Barebacking is an expression used to describe unprotected anal intercourse. Ever since the outbreak of AIDS over twenty-five years ago, the world of casual sex has changed forever, and the condom industry saw its biggest boom on record. Aside from abstinence, which is about as ridiculous to preach to gay men as it would be to ask them to stop listening to show tunes, the barrier method is the only way to avoid contracting HIV for those men who are not in a seronegative monogamous relationship. Unfortunately, history has taught us that not all gay men can follow these cold, hard rules. Instead, it has been shown over and over that men can be swayed by their sexual urges, which are often tainted by misinformation, alcohol, or drugs. The fact is that many gay men have an exorbitant amount of sex, and a fair percentage involves partners whom they hardly know. Yet despite the frequency, availability, and anonymity of sex, gay men still do not routinely ask the most essential question: "What is your HIV status?"

HIV has become a dividing line among gay men. Some HIV-positive men admit that if a new partner does not ask their status then they assume that he is positive. Alternately, some HIV negative men avoid asking about status because it ruins the mood. Considering both these situations exist, then why wouldn't it be logical to assume that everyone might be positive and that everyone should take the necessary precautions? Regrettably, this is not the case. Since the initial outbreak, gay men have struggled with this disease, and its impact on the community has been devastating. Generations around the globe have been wiped out because of AIDS, and regardless of the educational resources available in this country, gay men still engage in unsafe sex.

For some men it involves succumbing to the throes of passion as it relates to the desire for a human connection. Growing up in the closet, gay men learn to suppress their sexual urges, and when they are finally permitted to act on their desires, the potential exists to proceed without intellect. Another view is that unprotected sex is a reaction to the anger that accompanies internalized homophobia. Often barebacking is the result of actions that are hampered by alcohol, drugs, or both.

Directly correlated with the idea of barebacking are myths about HIV transmission. Some men refuse to use condoms as the insertive participant because it desensitizes the experience and this causes them to lose their erections. Often gay men foolishly believe that they can not contract HIV as the top. The facts are that HIV is a virus that is contracted through body fluids like semen or blood. It can be transmitted through both unprotected oral and recipient or insertive anal sex. Although unprotected recipient anal sex is the principle way that most gay men contract HIV, insertive partners are still at risk.

HIV is not the only unfortunate outcome that can be derived from barebacking. One must also consider the potential for gonorrhea, chlamydia, syphilis, and hepatitis B and C. It is well documented by the CDC that rates of syphilis as well as other STDs have increased exponentially over the past few years and this rise correlates directly with the number of new cases of HIV.

In the spring of 2005, the terms *supervirus* and *reinfection* were highly publicized in an issue of *New York* magazine. This cover story documented a single case of a man who had progressed to AIDS in just two months

Risk of HIV transmission for different kinds of exposures

EXPOSURE	RISK OF TRANSMISSION
RECEPTIVE ANAL INTERCOURSE	0.1 PERCENT—0.3 PERCENT (1/1,000—3/1,000)
INSERTIVE ANAL SEX	0.03 PERCENT (3/10,000)
INJECTION-NEEDLE SHARING	0.67 PERCENT (6.7/1,000)
ORAL SEX	0.01 PERCENT (1/10,000)

after contracting HIV. The impending threat that more gay men would be popping up with similar strains of this supervirus was never realized; however, it did shine a spotlight on the escalating crystal methamphetamine epidemic and the subsequent rise in barebacking among MSMs. Using gay Internet Web sites, men using the acronym PNP, which stands for "party and play," invite other men to engage in sex while using recreational drugs, especially crystal methamphetamine.

One important issue brought up by this article is the myth that among HIV-positive gay men, barebacking is safe because similar strains of HIV could not cause new risks to their health. To understand why this is a myth, you need to know that when HIV is exposed to antiretroviral medication, the virus can undergo a change and mutate. Once the virus mutates it then becomes resistant to certain drugs. If someone is HIV positive but does not have any mutations and barebacks with someone who does, then he could possibly inherit those mutations and as a result jeopardize the treatment. Developing mutations could limit treatment options.

In 2004 at the Eleventh Conference on Retroviruses and Opportunistic Infections held in San Francisco, investigators from Los Angeles and San Diego presented information on the incidence of sexually acquired superinfection. Their conclusion was that the annual rate of superinfection was 5 percent. This statistic does not apply to HIV-positive men who are on antiretroviral therapy. Superinfection is the re-infection of an HIV-positive person with a slightly different version or strain of HIV. The first documented report of it was in 2002, when researchers at the University of Geneva, Switzerland, presented a case study of a thirty-eight-year-old gay man who was infected with two different subtypes of HIV on two different occasions more than two-and-a-half years apart.

To add insult to injury, it was also noted that the co-infection rates of HIV and hepatitis B and C are escalating, with an estimated one third of HIV-positive patients co-infected with hepatitis C, and about 10 percent of HIV-positive patients having a chronic form of hepatitis B. More important is the fact that those patients who are co-infected with HIV and hepatitis C are less likely to respond to hepatitis C treatment compared to those who have hepatitis C alone. Also, the co-infected patient is more likely to be hit harder by the side effects while undergoing treatment for hepatitis C. Currently, the leading cause of hospitalization among co-infected patients is problems associated with hepatitis C. It has also been theorized that liver failure, not opportunistic infections, will be a leading cause of death in co-infected patients in the years to come.

Even more discouraging were recent reports by the CDC that rates of new HIV infections among gay men ages thirty-five to fifty are rising. It would appear unreasonable that this group of men who lived through the worst part of the epidemic and escaped uninfected would now submit to taking health risks. The explanation for this new occurrence is multifaceted.

Middle-aged gay men suffered tremendous losses during the 1980s due to AIDS. It was estimated that by the end of the decade the average gay man had lost six personal contacts to the disease. The survivors had higher rates of post-traumatic stress, and for some it was left untreated. Furthermore, the rates of depression and anxiety among gay men are twice as high compared to the general population. For those who have survived the epidemic, many find themselves lonely and isolated as many of their friends and family have disappeared. Combined with the psychological repercussions, many gay men resort to drugs and alcohol. It is well known that the crystal methamphetamine epidemic has wreaked havoc on gay men all over the country and has contributed more than its share of new cases of HIV. Some LGBT centers report that 10 to 30 percent of all new cases of HIV involve crystal methamphetamine.

Interestingly, there are a variety of psychosocial factors that contribute to why older gay men are now seroconverting. In addition to anxiety, depression, and drug use, many older gay men find themselves in a situation where they are dating younger men after having lost their lovers. These younger men who did not live through the epidemic have a completely different view of HIV. Some see it as a treatable disease with easy-to-take medications. The threat of death is not as haunting for these younger men. A case in point involves several older patients who were involved with younger men and found themselves going to circuit parties and partaking in casual three-ways as a way to keep up with their younger partners. Another began using anabolic steroids in an attempt to maintain his appearance and shared a needle with his HIV-positive partner. The examples go on and on but the reality is that older men are contracting HIV despite their age and wisdom. When confronted with the news of their status, many seem relieved. The rational that AIDS was bound to catch up with them at some point in their lives is a shared belief.

As a practitioner, the focus cannot be geared exclusively to prevention. All gay men must have some sense of how HIV is contracted. The problem lies with addressing health-care concerns for all gay men, especially as they pertain to psychosocial issues, depression and anxiety, and the fear over aging. AIDS cannot be viewed as an inevitable reality for all gay men.

HIV POST-EXPOSURE PROPHYLAXIS

In 1997 the CDC established a protocol for patients who had been exposed to HIV after unprotected sexual encounters called post-exposure prophylaxis, or PEP. The theory behind PEP is that HIV infection does not occur immediately after exposure. Once someone is exposed to the virus, it takes at least twenty-four to forty-eight hours before it reaches the lymph nodes and possibly days before it is active in the bloodstream. If the exposed individual is started on antiretroviral medication, the same used to treat HIV-positive patients, the proliferation of the virus may be prevented.

The CDC recommends that patients begin PEP within the first thirty-six hours after exposure. Individuals who think they may have been exposed to HIV should contact their doctor or report to their local emergency room as soon as possible. If your primary-care doctor or ER physician is unfamiliar with PEP, then you should find an HIV specialist or call the PEP hotline. The recommendation for PEP is reserved for high-risk exposures and should be instituted within the first few hours and not after the first 72 hours.

High-risk sexual activity

> *Receptive anal sex without a condom*
> *Performing oral sex and swallowing semen*
> *Insertive anal sex without a condom*
> *Fisting without a glove*
> *Rimming*

MY FIRST experience with PEP came after I had stuck myself with a needle while I was working in the ICU at Metropolitan Hospital. I was inserting an intravenous line into a comatose patient who was both HIV and hepatitis C positive. The needle went through his skin, then out and into my finger. I was wearing a latex glove but the gauge of the needle was so large that it went right through the glove and left a gaping hole in my skin. Luckily my senior resident knew about PEP and the urgency of getting me on treatment. I was taken to the emergency room, where I was given an HIV test, and then I was started on a triple-drug antiret-

Low-risk sexual activity

> *Kissing*
> *Mutual masturbation*
> *Oral sex without ejaculation*
> *Anal sex with a condom*
> *Fisting with a glove*
> *Rimming with a barrier*

roviral regimen that included Retrovir (AZT), Epivir (3TC), and Cixivan (indinavir). I was instructed to take these medications for twenty-eight days, and then I was told of their potential side effects, the main ones being nausea, vomiting, and diarrhea. Indinavir specifically can cause kidney stones, so I was warned to drink at least two liters of water a day. A follow-up appointment was made for me seventy-two hours later, when an infectious-disease fellow and I reviewed the PEP protocol again. More important, I was alerted to watch for signs or symptoms suggestive of HIV seroconversion. These viral symptoms mimic the flu, with fever, weakness, and coldlike symptoms. I took the pills for a total of twenty-eight days and I never seroconverted.

If you think you may have been exposed to the virus, ask your partner his HIV status. If he confirms your suspicions, try to ascertain his latest T-cell count, viral load, and current drug regimen. This information would be extremely valuable for your doctor in his decision-making process. Those patients who are deemed candidates for PEP are started on a regimen defined by the CDC, which may involve two to three drugs for a period of twenty-eight days. Baseline HIV testing should be done prior to instituting PEP. This is to ensure that candidates are not HIV positive already.

Clinicians who are familiar with PEP will discuss how to take the medication and what side effects to expect. It is important to follow up with your physician in order to review the PEP protocol and to monitor for signs and symptoms suggestive of HIV seroconversion.

These symptoms may include:

> *Fever*
> *Tiredness*
> *Body aches*
> *Cough*
> *Rash*
> *Headache*
> *Congestion*

If any of these symptoms develop while on PEP, immediately report to your doctor for HIV testing. In all other cases, individuals undergo repeat HIV testing at six and twelve weeks, and then again in six months. PEP is no "morning-after pill," which is a gross bastardization of a term that was derived from the FDA-approved medication called RU486, which is used to terminate pregnancy after unprotected vaginal sex. Both PEP and RU486 should never replace the barrier method as a way to avoid any sexually transmitted disease.

The CDC reports that one third of all cases of HIV in the United States are gay men, while as a whole they make up less then 10 percent of the population. These statistics back up anecdotal information that in major cities like New York City one out of every three gay men is HIV positive. With such statistics it becomes apparent that mixed couples or those in which one member is

HIV positive would become a reality for many gay men. Unfortunately, the information about mixed couples is only beginning to become available. Current statistics about mixed couples state that the risk of seroconversion is the same as it is for MSMs who don't know their partner's status. Some clinicians have made the argument that HIV negative members of a mixed couple are less likely to seroconvert because they are aware of the facts and take better precautions. Using condoms to ensure safety and the role of PEP have become a theme at most HIV conferences.

In 2006, scientists debated over PrEP or pre-exposure prophylaxis. This is instituting antiretroviral medication before engaging in high risk sexual behavior. Currently, the CDC is sponsoring several clinical trials including ones directly associated with PrEP, in an attempt to deal with the estimated 40,000 new people that are diagnosed with HIV annually. Per the CDC: "PrEP could help address the urgent need for a female-controlled prevention method for women worldwide who are unable, because of cultural and other barriers, to negotiate condom use. Furthermore, if effective, it could provide an additional safety net for all men and women at risk due to sexual or drug-using behaviors, when combined with reducing the number of sexual partners, HIV counseling and testing, condom use, use of sterile syringes, and other prevention measures." This concept is not new to physicians who have been treating patients prophylactically for infectious diseases associated with travel. Doctors have been pretreating patients for malaria before they arrive in endemic areas. The idea is that medication will already be in the bloodstream before the patient is exposed to a disease and prevent him from contracting it. Clinicians already know that a single dose of nevirapine given to women prior to labor and then to their newborn immediately after birth reduces the risk for mother-to-child transmission of HIV about 50 percent.

Even before PrEP was discussed publicly, a patient told me that he would use his partner's antiretroviral medication before sneaking off to a sex party as a precautionary practice. This was not an isolated case. Sex parties are a common occurrence fueled by Internet sex sites. Some hosts supply their guests with "party favors," that include an assortment of medications to correct erectile dysfunction, like Viagra, antiretrovirals, and recreational drugs, in order to facilitate the experience and heighten the sexual response. These combinations can have untoward effects when taken together, so please discuss them with your health care provider.

Dr. Frank's Tips on What to Do after Unsafe Sex

1. Ask your partner his HIV status.
2. Ask him his T-cell count, viral load, and what medications he is on.
3. Ascertain whether or not he ejaculated inside you.
4. Seek medical attention immediately! Preferably no more than 72 hours after the incident.

The concern over HIV is that the number of men infected has not declined. In fact, the CDC reported a 10 percent increase in the number of cases among MSMs from 2002 to 2006. "Although death is not as imminent as it was back at the onset of this epidemic, when I was going to a funeral a day," said Dr. Larry Higgins, "HIV is still a fatal disease." *Chronic* and *treatable* are more appropriate terms assigned to this disease. "Has the pendulum swung so far to the right that we've forgotten a time when gay men were dropping like flies?" asked Dr. Higgins. Neither PEP nor PrEP should ever replace the use of condoms. For further questions, consult your doctor or call the National Clinicians' Post-Exposure Prophylaxis Hotline (PEPline) at 888-HIV-4911 or the CDC's Web site at www.cdc.gov.

CHAPTER 9

Methicillin-Resistant *Staphylococcus Aureus*

IN LATE 2002, a bacterial outbreak occurred in Los Angeles affecting dozens of gay men. Then, in early 2003, reports described similar outbreaks in San Francisco. These cases were indicative of a growing phenomenon that had only been seen in the hospital setting up until this time. What was happening seemed reminiscent of the early days of the AIDS epidemic, but this time clinics serving gay men and HIV-positive people were describing a cluster of rashes caused by Methicillin-resistant *Staphylococcus aureus,* or MRSA.

Staphylococcus aureus, dubbed staph, is a common bacterium found on the skin and in the nose. Approximately 25 to 30 percent of Americans have staph, while 1 percent has MRSA. Infection results when the intact skin is disrupted and the bacterium is allowed to enter— for example, when men shave their body hair. Minor cuts and abrasions become a portal for bacteria to enter.

Easily treated with penicillin back in the 1940s, staph gradually developed resistance to the drug over the years, but it still retained sensitivity to the antibiotic methicillin. Drug resistance has become a major health-care concern. Inappropriate use of antibiotics is one of the major contributing factors to drug-resistant strains, especially in the hospital setting, where MRSA first emerged. This growing problem led to the Preservation of Antibiotic for Human Treatment Act of 2002. This bill was designed to promote public awareness of drug-resistant bacteria. In addition to doctors who overtreat viral illnesses, patients self-medicate, and this can result in drug resistance as well.

By early 2004, physicians in New York caring for mainly gay men began diagnosing more and more MRSA cases. By 2005, hundreds of men were showing up in doctors' offices and clinics with rashes caused by this voracious bacterium. It became a routine practice for health-care providers in major cities to empirically treat all their gay patients who present with rashes for MRSA. The exponential rise in numbers led the New York State board of health and the CDC to issue guidelines regarding treatment and prevention.

Transmitted through body contact, especially skin to skin during sex, MRSA can also be passed indirectly by touching contaminated gym equipment, towels, or sheets. Men who visited gyms and bathhouses were es-

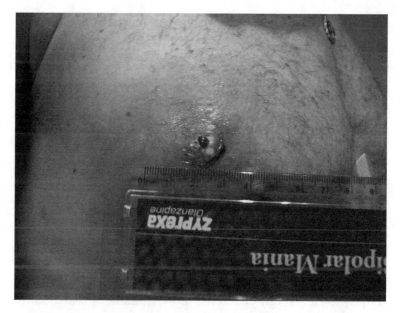

MRSA (Methicillin-Resistant Staphylococcus Aureus) infection of the chest
Photo by the author.

pecially at risk, with the additional use of saunas and Jacuzzis. The CDC issued five major factors contributing to transmission: close contact, crowding, cleanliness, contamination, and compromised skin. The issue with skin integrity is a major concern for gay men who often shave body parts. Compounded by the use of whirlpools and bathhouses, this added to the spread of MRSA.

Originally noted as a small area of redness, gay men were often ignoring these seemingly minor rashes, often dismissing them as bug bites. In time, however, the infected skin or cellulitis would progress quickly into tender pustules or small clusters of pimples referred to medically as abscesses or boils. In addition to these physical symptoms, fever and lethargy were also common.

Ignorance about MRSA was not reserved for gay men. Numerous emergency rooms and clinics across the country were misdiagnosing MRSA because the growing epidemic was not being publicized.

Complicating matters further was describing MRSA to gay men. The issue with being a carrier became important because after treatment, some people carry MRSA asymptomatically in their nose or rectum for days to months. In addition, analysis of these infected gay men showed an association with sex, drug use, and environmental exposure. Having multiple sex partners, meeting partners in sex clubs, bathhouses, on the Internet, and at sex parties, were all shown to increase the risk of acquiring MRSA. Condoms had a protective effect, as did prophylactic treatment with co-trimazole, while some recreational drugs such as crystal meth, poppers, and medications for erectile dysfunction were also reported to increase chances of infection. Likewise, it was found that men with HIV were more at risk for acquiring MRSA because of their increased exposure to hospital and clinic settings where MRSA was more likely to be found. Incidentally, immune status was not found to correlate with the risk of MRSA. Even men who used anabolic steroids had a greater risk due to the high prevalence of acne and inserting needles into their skin.

Diagnosing MRSA involves identification of the bacteria by culture and sensitivity. Often pus oozes from the infected area itself, and doctors can easily culture the fluid with a swab that is sent off to the lab. Proper identification of the organism is essential to treatment. If treatment is delayed, the infection can progress, traveling to the lymphatics and underlying muscle. This serious form of MRSA causes muscle breakdown, and hospitalization is required for intravenous antibiotics and surgical removal of dead tissue

Guidelines for the management and treatment of MRSA include performing an incision and drainage of any abscess. This is often the primary and only therapy for such infections, along with warm compresses. Expect your doctor to perform a culture of the abscess drainage. This will facilitate treatment by providing the doctor with the sensitivity of the organism to the appropriate antibiotic. Topical mupirocin, or Bactroban, may be used in less severe cases. Oral medications that are commonly prescribed include Bactrim DS (trimethoprim/sulfamethoxazole), which is frequently the most sensitive, as well as clindamycin, tetracycline, and linezolid. A combination with dual antibiotics—for example, trimethoprin/sufamethoxazole and rifampin—for a period of at least two weeks is the usual course of treatment.

Carriers of MRSA can include those who were treated and especially those with recurrent MRSA infections. If MRSA is allowed to colonize or collect on the skin or in the nose, this could lead to re-infection. In these cases, the recommended course of action is intranasal mupirocin applied to both nostrils twice a day for five days. This is done to decolonize gay men who have recurrent infections or those who are repeatedly exposed to MRSA. Other methods for decolonization include showers with a specific antimicrobial soap such as chlorhexidine for five days. In some cases, it is recommended that decolonization be offered to sexual partners or household contacts.

Severely ill patients with MRSA often appear very ill. These cases can also be complicated by the fact that the men suffer from other conditions, such as AIDS, heart disease, and diabetes. These patients require immediate evaluation by a clinician. Sepsis, a syndrome that includes fever and low blood pressure, and cases of limb or life-threatening infection requires hospitalization. These patients need broad spectrum antibiotics, such as intravenous vancomycin.

The aggressive nature of MRSA has resulted in severe cases that have required surgical removal of the infected area. Some gay men have even undergone skin grafts to aid the healing process because these infected areas are so large. Untreated cases have also progressed to involve infection of the underlying bone and have led to osteomyelitis, pneumonia, and bloodstream infections.

Dr. Frank's Tips on How to Avoid MRSA

1. Wash your hands thoroughly with soap and water.
2. At the gym, lay a towel down to avoid skin contact with gym equipment.
3. Limit the number of sex partners and wash thoroughly after sexual contact.
4. Avoid contact with other men's skin if it appears infected or contaminated.
5. If you think you have a suspicious rash, see your doctor immediately.

Tips on how to prevent others from getting it from you!

1. Keep the infected area covered. Pus from infected wounds contains active bacteria, so be sure to discard bandages and tape afterward.
2. Advise friends, family, and coworkers to maintain strict hand washing with good old soap and water. Better yet are those antibacterial liquids provided at gyms and certain public restrooms.
3. Avoid sharing personal hygiene accouchements—towels, razors, clothing, wash clothes, uniforms.
4. If you have been given an antibiotic regimen, be sure to complete the entire course even if the rash resolves sooner.
5. Clean and disinfect household surfaces and wash sheets and towels regularly.

CHAPTER 10

Modern Love: Monogamy, Three-Ways, and the Open Relationship

GAY RELATIONSHIPS have always held a curious fascination for society, especially now as homosexuals fight for their legal right to marry. Traditionally, gay men have fashioned their relationships according to heterosexual norms. Yet even for those men who had long-term monogamous role models, some gay men still find themselves struggling with sustaining their own relationships. In fact, whenever the topic of monogamy comes up among gay men, it is a subject for debate.

Certainly monogamy is a comforting concept. It incorporates traditional heterosexual ideals and promotes a strong sense of stability, but implementing monogamy into gay society has been fraught with concerns about its validity in modern gay culture. Monogamy for many is regarded as a romanticized version of what heterosexual marriage would be like—that for every man there is one woman and their union should last throughout their lives. Aside from the legal contract, the idea of marriage is heavily steeped in religious beliefs. Many middle-aged gay men of today grew up as youths who believed that one day they would get married to women, have children, and take care of a family. Negotiating this idea into a gay union has been difficult for some, while for others the transition has been smooth. The truth is that heterosexual marriage ends in divorce nearly 50 percent of the time. In spite of this fact, many gay men still require monogamy and wish to enter into a legal form of marriage.

Carmine, a fifty-three-year-old male, has been in a monogamous relationship with the same man for the past fifteen years. He insists that this was not a decision that they had discussed, but one that was just assumed from the very beginning. "I was born in Italy," he said. "I have old-fashioned beliefs. My lover is from a Polish family, and he was brought up in the same manner. We never knew any other lifestyle." It is comforting to see two gay men who can live happily in a long-term, monogamous relationship. On the other hand, there are many gay men who believe that one man is simply not feasible. These men argue that monogamy is unachievable. "One man cannot be everything," argued Keith. "It is too much to ask, and sex is just sex." Keith, who had been in an open relationship with his partner for five years, contends that they have had a mutual understanding from the very beginning. "I told my boyfriend at the start," he said. "I love you, but I also love cock." Since then he and his boyfriend have broken up, but he maintains that it had nothing to do with being in an open relationship. Additionally, Keith admitted that he and his partner had not had sex with each other for the twelve months prior to their breakup.

Keith's position is not uncommon. Sex viewed as perfunctory or simply as a way to fulfill a need is how many gay men explain why one man is not sufficient. In view of gay men's lifestyles, it is easy to see why some men would consider this to be true. Sex is readily available. Gay men can find sex almost anywhere—the gym, the supermarket, even at the local Home Depot. It seems as if wherever gay men congregate, sex is a possibility.

For many men, their sexuality is an integral part of their personality. Upon entering a party, David explained how he "sexes" up the room to see if there is anyone he would sleep with. If his options are limited, he might even consider lowering his standards or abandoning his plan completely. Sexualizing situations is instinctual for some gay men. For them, social interactions involve negotiating sex first. This can be substantiated by the number of gay men who are friends with people they have slept with first. Mating rituals and sexual play do not diminish the possibility of a friendship once an intimate connection is ruled out.

The need for gay men to be desired correlates with the pressure of having to attain an ideal about what gay men should look like. This can mean many things depending on what you view as sexy. This superficial desire, however, only temporarily sustains us. If you find that you require a lot of attention, or more than what is offered by your partner, then you might consider that you have issues with low self-esteem. This is common in gay men. Sometimes concern over one's sexiness can supersede all other accomplishments like career, education, or interests.

There are men who can see past the superficial and argue that what may appear to be sexy does not necessarily translate into a good sex partner. "I've slept with a ton of hot guys who were lame in bed," said Joe. "There has to be something more." Meanwhile, Carmine insists that good sex and monogamy can co-exist. He is emphatic that he and his partner maintain an active sex life that is made more meaningful because they love each other. Later Carmine admitted that he has had a few discreet encounters in the gym. "Strangers have initiated some playful touching in the shower," he said. "But I don't know if you consider that cheating."

The question of monogamy is dependant on whether you both have accepted the dynamic of the relationship or if you are truly falling into a role. Men who feel trapped by their relationships are more likely to cheat. Also, partners who feel that they are not able to talk openly without the threat of conflict also tend to stray. Cheating involves a violation of an agreement that is understood by both members of the couple. Others have made the argument that cheating can only exist if you get caught. This "tree falling in the woods cannot be heard" theory is Bobby's definition when confronted about an affair he was having behind his partner's back. They had been in a three-year relationship, and he had assumed openness about the future possibility of extramarital sex yet never discussed this with his partner. Bobby also crossed the line when he began to have deeper feelings for the other person. The result was that his partner, Rick, threw him out. Eventually the affair ended and Rick allowed Bobby to move back in. Their story typifies another segment of gay relationships. The search for something that is missing in a gay man's life or the need to fill an emptiness drives some into a desperate attempt to fill the void with sex.

For some couples, cheating is something that is understood but never discussed. These men opt for a "don't ask, don't tell" agreement. In deciding what works best for you, it is important to discuss this matter with your partner. Honesty about monogamy and open relationships is dependant upon you being honest with yourself.

Ask yourself, "What do I want from this relationship?"

Don't get caught up in thinking you should live a certain way because that was how you were brought up, and don't change your lifestyle because "this is the way it is in gay society." Having rules seems necessary; however, they always seem to get broken. Establishing boundaries implies a partnership and negotiating them establishes trust within the couple. The two of you should come to some sort of agreement that works best for both, even if it is something your friends frown upon. Whether it is a "don't ask, don't tell," arrangement, monogamy, or a completely open relationship, this is something both partners need to be in agreement with. If there is any apprehension, then it is up to you to tell your partner. Don't be afraid to slow down. There is nothing more detrimental to a relationship than an apprehensive partner moving too quickly into an open one.

There are a variety of different versions of the open relationship. On the one hand, some couples choose to invite a third party, which is called a three-way. Usually the intention is to spice up their sex life by adding a third or even another couple. Discussing your expectations prior to a three-way allows both partners to express any concerns they might have. Rich and Peter have been together for nearly twenty years. They have been exploring sex with other men for a good portion of their relationship. "We were monogamous for the first five years," said Peter. "The sex was great, but after a while it became a little monotonous." After a lengthy discussion, they both agreed on having a three-way. "The intention was to just have fun," said Rich. "There was nothing missing from our relationship." His point is well taken. I have heard horror stories about what happens after a couple opens their relationship. For some the lust for sex takes precedence over the relationship and breaking up becomes just another acceptable consequence. "Mutual respect and love is all that we ask of each other," said Peter. "Besides, I always get to choose."

For many the three-way is more a necessity than an outlet. It allows the partners to engage in sexual acts that they might not necessarily enjoy performing with each other. The important thing to remember is that the invited guest leaves after a three-way, and you are left with your partner afterward. Be sure to pay attention and look for signs that might suggest he is not participating. A good idea is to discuss with your partner what is and is not acceptable before the three-way. Some men are very specific about what they will allow their partner to do during a three-way. One couple disclosed that kissing on the mouth was not allowed, while another was clear that neither could be penetrated by a third. Too many restrictions or rules can be a warning sign that your partner is not ready to venture into the world of the open relationship. If this is the case, then it would be prudent for you to discuss these matters with your partner before proceeding. It is a very slippery slope from desire to despair. Make sure you both have a good understanding of what you are getting yourselves into. Be cognizant of your own feelings, and be prepared to share your partner with someone else. The best-case scenario is one in which everyone is satisfied.

"That rarely happens," said Joe. "Usually the third party is really only into one of the guys in the couple and the other inevitably feels left out."

This is a very real possibility. That is why it is so important for couples to verbalize or signal each other when one is feeling excluded. A good rule could be that if, at any time during the three-way, one partner does not wish to continue, then the arrangement is called off. However, some couples have learned to make certain allowances when one member has a stronger connection with the third. In these situations, the odd man out allows his partner to enjoy himself without the threat of guilt. Such is the case with Ted and Jim, a couple in their late forties. They have been together for nine years and thoroughly enjoy three-ways. Jim said that they both have different tastes, and on occasion he has allowed Ted some liberty with the third party. Ted agreed. "Sometimes if I feel that Jim is having fun and I am not really into it, then I will leave the two of them alone," he said. "It is understood that every three-way is not going to be satisfying for everyone, every time."

Even if there is an underlying fear or apprehension, couples who insist on participating in an open relationship prefer three-ways to the alternative. Exploring sexual relationships without your partner's presence is another version of the open relationship, and one that some couples find more suitable. "I don't want to see him

THIS PAST year, a courageous gay couple acquired the help of a surrogate to carry their child. This baby was created from the purchase of a donor egg, which was fertilized with the sperm of one of the males and then implanted into the surrogate. This couple's success seemed unprecedented, and it was a catalyst for a plan to have another child using the sperm of the other male. By using the same egg donor, the children will be related. Their remarkable achievement involved quite a bit of money and a substantial commitment to parenthood.

At their annual Christmas party, I met their beautiful new daughter. Incidentally, this couple recently opened their relation-

getting fucked," said William. "Besides, I hate three-ways. I'm always more concerned with wondering if everyone is all right, and I don't get to enjoy myself." The intensity derived from a sexual encounter with someone other then your spouse is something that some men find very exhilarating. This experience is only heightened if it is limited to just two people. Still some men who prefer this version of the open relationship contend that they are not excluding their partners because they find shar-

ship to include another man they met abroad. He was coming to stay with them through the New Year and was going to join them in celebrating the holidays with their extended family. Knowing that they were both raised in a traditional Catholic household, I wondered how they were going to explain the presence of the guest to their parents.

Later they confessed how nervous they were that day. "My father was so excited because it was the baby's first Christmas and in walks Gabriel with us," he said. "My father just looked at me like, 'Who the hell is this?' Due to the excitement of the day, there was no request for us to explain who this new man was, and dinner went on as usual."

ing the experience with them afterward very erotic. "It makes me feel good to see my boyfriend getting hit on," said William. "And I like to hear the details about it later. I just don't want to be there." There are gay men who find their partners' extra-marital encounters thoroughly stimulating. For others the thought of their partners having sex with others is disturbing, and this concern should always be explored because if jealously occurs, this could potentially develop into something more detrimental to the relationship.

WHEN MY SISTER and her family arrived this past holiday, I found myself a little envious. Her children have finally come to that age where I can really appreciate them. Over the course of their young lives, I have held my breath patiently waiting for the day when they would first discover that their uncle was gay. My first hint was when the eldest, Matthew, shot a look at his mother when I recommended that they see a movie called *Little Miss Sunshine.* "You'll love it," I said and then added without realizing, "There is even a gay Uncle Frank in it." That look of recognition on my nephew's face told me that he was already aware of my sexuality. Then I began to worry if he was embarrassed, and suddenly I was flooded with memories of what it was going to be like if I had to "come out" all over again. After a certain age, some gay men shrug off any anxiety associated with having to admit their sexuality. More so in the social setting; however, in clinical practice, many of my older gay patients have found cause for concern when being referred to specialists. The process of coming out all over again seems unsettling and is another reason that I chose to associate myself with gay doctors or ones who are gay-friendly.

Dr. Frank's Relationship Tips

1. Talk. Don't be afraid to tell him what you want. Be open and honest without being rude. If he doesn't want to listen, that's his problem.
2. Listen. Let him tell you what is on his mind without fear of being criticized. You should be his friend. Allow him to express himself in an environment that is safe and not hostile.
3. Boundaries. As your relationship evolves, set limits about what you both expect in the relationship. Setting goals as a couple allows you to unite as partners toward a specific outcome.
4. Expectations. No one wants to be disappointed, but in reality it is inevitable. Be realistic about what you expect from each other. No one is perfect, and if you can live with his flaws, then perhaps he will be able to make concessions about yours.
5. Outcomes. Always treat each other with respect. Never let anyone else know something about your relationship that you haven't discussed with your partner first. He should be in the loop at all times.

Some couples can maintain a relationship and explore their sexual boundaries; however, this must be determined on an individual basis. Homosexual unions end in "divorce" with as much frequency as their heterosexual counterparts. The exploration of how two men can co-exist relies on how committed they are to the relationship. Good relationships are built upon a solid foundation of mutual understanding. For some, establishing a family means having children. For others, it means taking on a third male.

The three-way relationship has become an interesting phenomenon in the gay community. Concerns over intimacy, sex, and family have been redefined in gay culture, especially with the fight for same-sex marriage and the exponential rise in gay adoption. Not since the outbreak of the AIDS crisis have homosexuals found cause to demand civil liberties. More and more, gay men have been taking on the role of parent with the help of adoption and surrogate mothers.

Gay men define family by their attachments to other members of their inner circle, whether blood-related, genetically created, or socially integrated. Discovering a sense of family has given many men a renewed sense of optimism about the fate of gay families. As gay families continue to evolve and involve other people in their world, it is important to hold on to traditional ideas of respect, love, and communication.

CHAPTER 11

Hypogonadism, Andropause, and Erectile Dysfunction

HYPOGONADISM

The AIDS crisis brought attention to many unknown issues involving gay health. With it we saw the ravages it brought to millions of men, women, and children around the globe, but it was also the impetus for an amazing amount of research that focused on health concerns that had been underserved up until then. One area in particular is HIV's effects on testosterone levels in men.

Among HIV-positive men the rate of hypogonadism—a clinical syndrome that results in a failure of the testes to produce testosterone within the normal range—increases with the progression of the disease and affects approximately 50 percent of men with HIV. It is estimated that in the United States nearly 13 million men suffer from low testosterone.

The male sex hormone, testosterone, is produced by the testes in a complex network called the hypothalamic-pituitary-gonadal axis, which involves the brain, the pituitary gland, and the testes. The hypothalamus, located just above the brain stem, secretes hormones that act to stimulate or inhibit the secretion of pituitary hormones. The pituitary gland sits in a bony cavity called the "sella turcica" and acts in conjunction with the hypothalamus to regulate physiological homeostasis. One of its functions is to maintain sex-hormone production in men and women. Specifically in men it acts to regulate the release of testosterone by the testes.

Testosterone is responsible for:

> *Sex drive and sexual function*
> *Muscle mass and strength*
> *Mood and energy levels*

Hypogonadism is also defined as low-serum testosterone. The average testosterone for a healthy adult male is between 240 and 820 ng/dl. Due to the large range most clinicians take the median, which falls between 400 and 500 ng/dl, as the true average. Men with levels below this range and those who present with symptoms suggestive of low testosterone are treated for hypogonadism.

In adults, hypogonadism can cause:

> *Erectile dysfunction*
> *Infertility*
> *Anemia*
> *Loss of muscle mass*
> *Loss of bone mass (osteoporosis)*

Masculine features attributed to normal testosterone can be altered with hypogonadism, leading to a decrease in body hair growth, small testicle size, and development of breasts. In addition, low testosterone can cause severe fatigue, loss of libido (decreased sex drive), and negative mood defined as anger, irritability, sadness, or depression.

There are two types of hypogonadism—primary and secondary. In primary hypogonadism, the problem lies with the testicles themselves and can be attributed to genetic disorders, viral infections like the mumps, trauma, aging, and cancer. With secondary hypogonadism, there is a defect in the brain affecting either the hypothalamus or the pituitary gland. Common secondary causes, especially in gay men, include anabolic steroid use, exogenous testosterone use, and HIV.

Hypogonadism in men with HIV is an ongoing concern, even in those patients who are stable on antiretroviral medication. That is because the virus affects the hypothalamic-pituitary axis. After the initial outbreak, it was found that men, especially those who had signs and symptoms of wasting, also had low testosterone. This was proof that signals to the testes were being disrupted. However, it was found that not all hypogonadal HIV-positive men had wasting, and conversely positive men with wasting did not necessarily have low testosterone.

Wasting and hypogonadism can occur independently of each other.

Treating HIV-positive men for hypogonadism has become a common practice. Testosterone replacement therapy comes in two forms. One is injectable and the other is a gel. Using cypionate testosterone, an oil-based solution, the medication is injected into the buttock at regular intervals. You either have it done at your doctor's office or inject yourself at home, usually every seven to fourteen days depending on your response. Over the years, the technology for testosterone replacement has advanced so that now men can apply a simple gel once a day to clean, bare, dry skin on the upper arms, shoulders, or abdomen. The gel eliminates the office visit and gives you more autonomy. One major difference is that it has to be applied every day. Brand-names such as Androgel and Testim have the advantage of offering sustained amounts of testosterone as opposed to the injections, which release a surge of the hormone. Also, with the injection, the levels peak immediately and then dwindle over time so that by the time the next shot is due, men experience a decrease in mood and energy level. Some men admit to experiencing extreme highs and lows. With the gel, there is more of a plateau because the medication is given daily. Men using the gel typically have consistent testosterone values, as opposed to men who use the injectable form, who also often experience more side effects due to higher levels.

ANDROPAUSE

An age-related decline in testosterone is normal in all men. In fact, testosterone levels show a huge drop by age seventy, and like women who undergo menopause usually by age fifty, men undergo a similar phase called andropause. Like menopause, andropause is associated with physical and emotional changes that can be alleviated by hormone replacement. Overall, 30 percent of men in their sixties and more than 80 percent of men in their eighties are found to have low testosterone levels. The decline in testosterone is gradual with a decrease of about 1 percent a year starting as early as age thirty. However with such a slow rate of decline, most men do not notice any symptoms until they are fifty.

In order to make the diagnosis of hypogonadism, a thorough review of symptoms should be established. These can include loss of libido, depression, and lethargy, but it's important to establish if they relate to some other underlying medical condition. A recent study concluded that men with certain conditions may be more likely to have low testosterone. If you have any of the following conditions and feel tired, depressed, or have a lack of sexual desire, then you may be suffering from low testosterone. These medical conditions include:

> *Obesity*
> *Diabetes*
> *High blood pressure*
> *High cholesterol*
> *Asthma/COPD especially with chronic steroid use*

The next step in diagnosing hypogonadism is to measure the total testosterone level in the blood. This test should be drawn in the morning when testosterone levels are at their highest, and then repeated at least once more to ensure accuracy. Testosterone levels less than 200 ng/dl are consistent with testosterone deficiency.

Levels between 200 ng/dl and 400 ng/dl are borderline deficient. Most doctors agree that measuring free testosterone under these conditions is valuable to evaluate the amount circulating freely in your blood.

According to the *Journal of Clinical Endocrinology and Metabolism*, testosterone replacement therapy is indicated for symptomatic men with low testosterone to induce and maintain sex characteristics, improve sexual function, muscle mass, bone mineral density, and overall sense of well-being. The most important stipulation is that men with a history of prostate or breast cancer should *not* undergo testosterone replacement therapy. It has been suggested that the progression of these cancers can be accelerated by increased levels of this hormone.

Before initiating replacement therapy, it is recommended that all men be screened for prostate cancer using a baseline blood prostate specific antigen, or PSA. Men with elevated PSAs (above 3 ng/mL) should not be started on testosterone replacement therapy until further urological evaluation. Also, those men who are given hormone replacement therapy should have PSAs checked routinely, at least every six months. New hormones called selective androgen receptor modulators (SARMs), which resemble testosterone but do not affect the prostate, are under development. Theoretically, these SARMs could offer the benefits of conventional testosterone therapy and significantly decrease the potential harmful side effects of the therapy.

Once testosterone therapy has been instituted, the recommendation is to maintain testosterone levels in the midnormal range, and men receiving therapy should be monitored using a standardized plan. Persistent high levels of testosterone will increase your risk for side effects including:

> *acne*
> *an increase in the number of red blood cells*
> *elevated PSAs*
> *impaired urination*
> *increased lipids*

In situations where men present with erectile dysfunction (ED), they should also be evaluated for hypogonadism. It is important to remember that ED and low testosterone are two distinctly separate medical issues that can co-exist, especially in older men.

ERECTILE DYSFUNCTION

Erectile dysfunction, or impotence, is the inability to gain or maintain an erection for the purpose of sex. ED affects 15 to 30 million American men, and many medical problems can affect a man's ability to sustain an erection. Common ones include cardiovascular disease, peripheral vascular disease, and diabetes. Even some highly common types of medications have an effect on erectile function, especially some antidepressants and medications that lower blood pressure. Other causes include psychological factors and issues concerning performance anxiety and depression.

Important questions to ask yourself regarding ED include:

> *Do you wake up with morning erections?*
> *Are you able to sustain an erection for penetration?*
> *Do you have decreased sexual thoughts?*
> *Are you able to ejaculate despite an inability to sustain a full erection?*

An erection has two phases: One is the direct stimulation of the penis, and the other is psychogenic, based on erotic stimuli. Physiologically, erectile stimulation leads to the release of nitric oxide, which causes the muscles of the main erectile tissue of the penis to relax. The penis then engorges with blood and an erection is produced. An adequate amount of testosterone must be present for an erection to take place. Impotence occurs when there is hormonal deficiency, disruption of the neural pathway, or an inadequate blood supply to the penis. Other causes can include post-surgical procedures, especially operations involving the prostate, or excessive alcohol or drug use. ED has also been linked to prolonged bicycle and horseback riding.

Treatment of ED depends on the cause. Testosterone replacement therapy is recommended for symptomatic men with low testosterone due to hypogonadism or androgen deficiency. ED that results from inadequate blood flow to the penis caused by damaged blood vessels is strongly associated with diabetes and peripheral vascular disease. Tight control of blood sugar is essential to maintain competency of blood vessels. Uncontrolled diabetics run the risk of damaging their vascular network, which can result in problems with the kidneys, eyes, and circulation to the extremities.

Medications indicated for the treatment of ED include Viagra (sildenafil), Cialis (tadalafil), and Levitra (vardenafil). Taken orally, these medications work by producing smooth muscle relaxation of the corpus cavernosum. The response is mediated by the release of nitric oxide, which results in increased blood flow and an erection. With the exception of testosterone replacement, these medications work on a temporary basis. They enable an erection to be attained and maintained long enough for intercourse but do not improve any underlying medical conditions. These medications treat ED; they do not cure it.

For most men, the average time to an erection is thirty to sixty minutes after ingesting the pill. All three medications require stimulation like kissing or touching. Among the most common side effects are headache, nasal congestions, flushing, and in some instances visual disturbances. More serious side effects include low blood pressure, irregular heart rate, and priapism. Men should not take these medications if they use nitrates, which can be found in certain chest pain medications (sublingual nitro) or amyl nitrite (poppers) for recreational use. The combined effect can severely lower blood pressure.

Used appropriately, these drugs have been widely successful, especially in older men with medical problems such as diabetes and hypertension. It is important to discuss your general health with your physician before using any of these medications in order to establish if you are healthy enough to engage in sexual activity. Remember to provide your doctor with a complete list of all your medications, especially blood pressure medications. Consult your doctor immediately if you develop chest pain or discomfort during sex and avoid further use. In cases of priapism or prolonged erections for longer then four hours, seek medical attention immediately.

Some clinicians have made the argument that these medications promote unsafe sex, especially among gay men, leading to increased cases of HIV. This concern has never been substantiated, but some MSMs do use recreational drugs that require ED medication to facilitate their sexual activity. The apprehension is that recreational drugs impair judgment and some gay men take part in long marathons of sex due in part to the aid of these ED medications. In light of these facts, it is important to note that Cialis has a half-life of 36 hours. Again, remember to always use condoms during sex and note that ED medications do not protect against STDs or HIV. Even more important, know that the use of amyl nitrite, or "poppers," with ED drugs is contraindicated. Taken together, they can have detrimental effects on blood pressure, leading to loss of consciousness and even death.

Previous medications used to treat ED came in the form of a urethral suppository under the brand name Muse (medicated urethral system for erection), which employs a prostaglandin pellet that is inserted into the urethra with an applicator. Said to be effective in 30 to 60 percent of the men who use it, the onset of action is about ten minutes after insertion and lasts anywhere from thirty minutes to an hour. Reported side effects include pain and urethral injury.

Other forms of prostaglandins were initially injectable under the brand names Caverject or Edex. This medication is injected into the side of the penis (the corpus cavernosum), producing erections in 80 percent of the men. The injections are relatively painless; the erection begins five to fifteen minutes after the injection. It is recommended that self-injection be performed no more than once every four to seven days. Side effects include infection, bleeding, and bruising at the injection site, dizziness, heart palpitations, and flushing. There is a risk for priapism, a medical emergency. Repeated injection may cause scarring of erectile tissue, which can further impair erection.

Priapism is a condition that involves a sustained erection beyond four hours and is a reported side effect of medical treatments for ED. In Greek mythology, the god Priapus was punished for attempting to rape a goddess by being given a large set of useless wooden genitals. The medical condition named after him is highly serious and requires immediate medical care.

One case of priapism involved a gay male who had a three-way with a couple that convinced him to inject prostaglandin into his penis. The ensuing erection continued for well past four hours before he went to his local emergency room. After a sustained erection, the blood within the penis becomes entrapped. Imagine having a tourniquet tied around the base of your penis. If the blood is not permitted to drain, it can clot, causing further swelling and permanent damage. Treatment involves aspirating the blood using a needle that is inserted into the penis. Phenylephrine can be injected as well to dilate the blood vessels. If medical treatment fails, surgical shunts are inserted.

Other methods used to achieve erections involve vacuum pumps. The penis is inserted into a device and a hand-held pump is used to create a vacuum that draws blood into the penis. Adequate erections have been reported after one to three minutes. The penis is then removed from the pump and a rubber ring is placed around the base to maintain the erection during intercourse. The ring can be left on for up to thirty minutes.

When all other measures have been exhausted there are always surgical alternatives. The three main surgical avenues include penile implants, vascular reconstructive surgery, and venous ligation.

Penile implants involve surgically inserting malleable rods or inflatable tubes into the penis. The malleable prosthesis provides rigidity sufficient for intercourse and can be curved downward so that it is concealed. The inflatable prosthesis consists of two tubes that are inserted into the penis and attached to a small pump implanted in

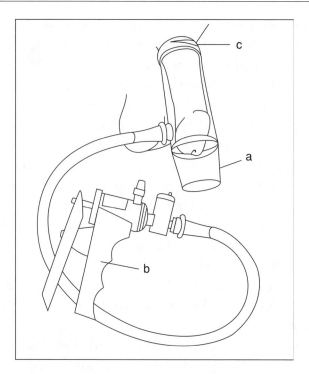

A vacuum-constrictor device causes an erection by creating a partial vacuum around the penis, which draws blood into the corpora carenosa. The necessary components illustrated here are: (a) a plastic cylinder, which covers the penis; (b) a pump, which draws air out of the cylinder that covers the penis; and (c) an elastic ring, which, when fitted over the base of the penis, traps the blood and sustains the erection after the cylinder is removed.

the scrotum. In order to produce an erection, the patient must manually pump fluid stored in a reservoir located in the abdomen. This acts to expand the penis so that it is erect. Afterward, a valve allows the fluid to return to the reservoir so that the penis can deflate. The surgical procedure to implant the inflatable prosthesis is slightly more complicated than the semi-rigid implant. Also, the inflatable prosthesis has a higher risk of mechanical failure.

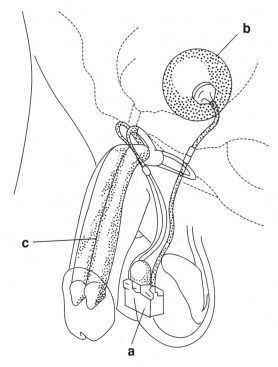

A Penile Implant
With an inflatable implant, erection is produced by squeezing a small pump (a) implanted in a scrotum. The pump causes fluid to flow from a reservoir (b) residing in the lower pelvis to cylinders (c) residing in the penis. The cylinders expand to create the erection.

Some vascular problems that cause ED can be treated surgically. A small percentage of men undergo vascular reconstructive surgery to improve blood flow to the penis. Bypassing blocked veins or arteries involves transferring a vein from the leg and attaching it so that it creates a path to the penis around the area of blockage. Young men with only local arterial blockage are the best candidates for this procedure. The procedure is almost never successful in older men with widespread blockage.

Venous ligation involves performing surgery on veins to allow blood to leave the penis. Blocking off veins, or ligating them, allows an adequate amount of blood to remain in the penis. Long-term effectiveness has been brought into question and as a result this procedure is rarely performed.

In addition to erectile dysfunction, some men suffer from ejaculatory problems like premature ejaculation. This is defined as ejaculation prior to one's wishes. This broad definition avoids a specific duration of time. Most men reach climax in five minutes, which is considered satisfactory. Other males have learned to delay their climax for up to twenty minutes and longer. If premature ejaculation occurs on occasion, it is not considered a cause for concern. However, if premature ejaculation continues for more than 50 percent of attempted sexual relations, a dysfunctional pattern probably exists.

Premature ejaculation is the most common male sexual dysfunction. In the United States, it affects approximately one out of five men aged eighteen to sixty. In gay men, premature ejaculation is thought to be related to psychological causes. Some clinicians agree that early sexual experiences, especially those in which men had to rush in order to climax in order to avoid being discovered, can set a lifelong pattern. Households that regard gay sex as sinful or dirty exacerbate this condition because the male tends to rush through sex in order to avoid feeling guilt.

If you suffer from premature ejaculation, consult your doctor. There are also biological factors that can contribute. Treatments include the use of antidepressants as well as sexual therapy and individual psychotherapy.

Delayed ejaculation refers to an inability to climax. The male is unable to ejaculate, either during intercourse or with manual stimulation in the presence of a partner. Sometimes he is able to ejaculate but only with great effort. Common causes are mainly psychological in nature and are the result, once again, of either a strict religious upbringing or traumatic childhood events. Closeted gay men develop ejaculatory problems especially during intercourse with female partners. Lack of attraction to one's partner is another common cause as well as an underlying anger as it relates to internalized homophobia. There are a variety of medications that can cause delayed ejaculation, including some common antidepressants. Neurological disease such as strokes or nerve damage to the spinal cord or back may also cause a delay in or an inability to ejaculate.

Erectile and ejaculatory dysfunction is also age-related, and other medical problems can exacerbate these conditions. Maintaining adequate sugar control in diabetics and normalizing blood pressure in hypertensive males is the best way to decrease your chance of erectile or ejaculatory problems. Also, excessive alcohol and recreational drugs have been implicated as causes for these two conditions as well.

PART III

Gay
Culture

CHAPTER 12

Recreational Drugs and the Party Circuit

THE CLUB scene and its association with recreational drugs is as much a part of gay culture as HIV. The party scene has been written about extensively in such wonderful books as Andrew Holleran's *Dancer From the Dance*, which describes in vivid detail the effects of drugs and dancing on gay men in New York City during the 1970s. Also, Michelangelo Signorile's *The Life Outside* gives a brilliant account of life on the "circuit," and how this drug-fueled world has defined an aesthetic for gay men. The pressure to conform to the distorted view of the gay male body image has forced some gay men to take extreme measures leading to drug addiction, depression, and AIDS.

The origin of the gay party circuit is difficult to pin-point. Although some suggest that vacation destinations like the Fire Island tea dances sparked the first of such annual parties, others refute this. Gay men congregated on occasions like mutual birthdays or anniversaries to celebrate their individuality and freedom from the homo-phobic world. These events evolved over the years and grew in number, especially once promoters recognized their value. Eventually these events became mega-parties and gay men flocked to them from all over the world.

Initially, the intention of these dance parties was to create an atmosphere for gay men to socialize. The addi-tion of recreational drugs acted to lower inhibitions and provoked an incredible sexual response. For example, the now-infamous Saint, a gay dance club made popular in the 1980s, attracted throngs of gay men because of its reputation for innovative house music and amazing tech-nical achievements that revolutionized the party experi-ence. For some, the Saint is regarded as the birth of the circuit party.

Currently, circuit parties consist of elaborate events hosted by resident drag queens with chart-topping artists and acrobatic performances that rival Cirque d'Soleil. Sometimes these events consist of parties that can go on for over twelve hours, with consecutive parties stretch-ing out over several days. In addition to the main event, which usually goes on past dawn, there are after-parties that extend into the afternoon. The intention for some men is to attend multiple parties in one extended week-end, staying up for unhealthy periods of time without rest or nutrition. In order to sustain their alertness, par-tygoers have turned to stimulants for help.

Throughout the 1980s and 1990s, the gay party scene escalated to include the growing demand for bigger parties and better highs. Club kids ushered in "raves," or underground dance parties, where ecstasy—the "love drug"—along with Special K (ketamine) made its name for its euphoric effects. But the combination of dance, drugs, and sex also hit a major setback once the AIDS epidemic hit. In addition to the overnight dance parties, sex clubs, bathhouses, and bars added to the increasing numbers of STDs and HIV infections. Gay men fell into a false sense of security by allowing themselves to be lured into unprotected sex due in part to recreational drugs. The combination of dance, drugs, and sex hit a major setback once the AIDS epidemic hit.

As the AIDS epidemic passed its peak, the gay party scene was resurrected, with gay men partying even harder and looking stronger thanks to anabolic steroids, which were intended to treat HIV-positive men suffering from wasting. Gary, a fifty-seven-year-old patient, who battled through the worst part of the epidemic, worked the system by selling his expensive and highly coveted growth hormone in order to supplement his income and his party habits. Examples like his were not few and far between and forced many clinicians into rethinking their treatment and prescribing habits. Over twenty-five years later, gay men are still becoming infected with HIV and life on the party circuit continues to grow on a global scale.

Even as life on the circuit attracts younger men, there are still older diehards who continue their party habits. Ralph and his twenty-five-year-old partner, James, continue to party, despite Ralph's heart attack in 2001. James, who is fifteen years his junior, does not support the suggestion that they need to curtail their habits in light of his own alcohol dependence and peptic ulcer disease. Clinicians who treat gay men who use recreational drugs, anabolic steroids, and alcohol are faced with moral, legal, and ethical dilemmas. How do you begin to treat someone you know is abusing his body?

"I don't," said one clinician. "I won't even hear about it. When they tell me they use drugs or steroids, I tell them to find a new doctor." Most other gay health-care providers are less rigid and encourage their patients to be honest. Only when patients are presented with the facts are they able to make well-informed decisions.

ECSTASY

MDMA, or 3, 4-methylenedioxy-N-methylamphetmaine, is commonly known as ecstasy, X, or XTC. It has often been referred to as the "love drug" because it stimulates the secretion of serotonin, a neurotransmitter that induces a sense of euphoria, energy, and openness. Absorption of serotonin as well as dopamine and norepinephrine is inhibited by its use and so increased amounts of these neurotransmitters flood the brain. Users experience a heightened sense of emotion, generalized happiness, and tactile stimulation.

First synthesized in 1912 in Germany, it was used in the 1970s in conjunction with psychotherapy because its effect on lowering inhibitions was a powerful tool as a way to break through psychological barriers. Later, in the 1980s, MDMA began to be used for nonmedical purposes because of its psychedelic effects. In 1985, the Drug Enforcement Agency (DEA) made MDMA illegal.

Gay men popularized ecstasy use in the early 1980s, often combining it with other recreational drugs like cocaine, alcohol, Special K, and crystal methamphetamine. Due to the increased sense of pleasure, ecstasy was often used in dance clubs to heighten the musical experience and promote socialization. "Rolling," or taking ecstasy, became a phenomenon especially among those who went to all-night raves or dance parties.

The down side is that ecstasy can mask underlying exhaustion as users continue to party for prolonged periods of times without rest. In addition, it causes extreme elevations in temperature (hyperthermia) and results in dehydration, especially when sufficient amounts of water are not ingested. Prolonged exposure to high temperatures also results in muscle breakdown, or rhabdomyolysis, which can lead to kidney failure. Conversely, there are also documented cases of water intoxication as some users overhydrate, resulting in low sodium or hyponatremia. There have also been documented cases of this causing seizures and death. Along with episodes of elevated blood pressure are documented cases of liver failure. Combining ecstasy with Norvir (ritonovir), a widely used drug for HIV, was responsible for the death of at least one gay man due to the interference of the liver's ability to metabolize these drugs.

The most common side effect of ecstasy use is depression after the drug wears off. "Suicide Tuesday" is the common term partygoers use to describe the ensuing depression after a weekend binge on ecstasy. This is primarily due to the brain's serotonin depletion. Long-term effects of chronic ecstasy use include prolonged depression. Other common side effects include bruxism, or teeth grinding, which deteriorates the tooth's enamel and can result in jagged or chipped teeth. Also trismus, or clenched jawed, can occur.

Purchased on the street, ecstasy comes in a pill form and is taken orally. Often partygoers take more than one pill in the course of a night out clubbing. Accounts suggest that in addition to oral consumption, some men insert the pill in their anus, which is commonly referred to as the "booty bump." The rich blood supply of the anal mucosa causes quick absorption. Similarly, some ingest one pill and insert the other in their anus for a "train wreck," in order to accelerate the drug's response and cause a flood of serotonin.

Pills are individualized according to color and often monogrammed with a specific symbol. Various signs include logos, initials, or other insignias like smiley faces in order to characterize a specific batch of ecstasy. Since colors and symbols are easy to duplicate, there is no way to ensure that a specific pill was produced in a previously known batch.

Sales of ecstasy have become an increasingly profitable business, with pills costing anywhere from fifteen to thirty dollars each. Due to the profitability and escalating cost of MDMA production, the amount of MDNA used differs from one supplier to the next. Often makers substitute cheaper byproducts in their production or cut their ecstasy with cheaper forms of speed and opioids. There was a time when certain not-for-profit organizations were testing individual pills for quality to assure that whoever was taking them would at least be aware of what the main ingredients were. Nowadays it is rare to find pure MDMA.

Ecstasy has become so widespread that the National Survey on Drug Use estimated that roughly 450,000 people used it in 2004 alone. Although death due to ecstasy is difficult to estimate, the DEA reported that over 5,000 people were brought to the emergency room in 2003. Of these patients, only seventy-six died due to MDMA alone. This number, however, is thought to be underestimated due to the high propensity of fatalities due to multiple drugs on board at the time of death.

Treatment for chronic users focuses on behavioral modification and lifestyle changes. Clinicians have had moderate success treating the depressant effects of ecstasy with selective serotonin re-uptake inhibitors, or SSRIs. Since MDMA depletes the brain of serotonin, neurons are unable to function properly. This results in depression. SSRIs act to slow down the process of returning serotonin to the neuron it comes from, and this leaves the chemical in the vicinity of the receptor for a prolonged period of time. As the level of serotonin builds up, this sets off an impulse to the next neuron. SSRIs work by allowing the body to make the best use of the reduced amounts of serotonin it has. Over a period of time, the levels of natural serotonin will rise again (as long as MDMA use is discontinued), and the SSRI can be reduced and eventually withdrawn.

KETAMINE

Ketamine, or Special K, Kitty, or Vitamin K is a common anesthetic used among veterinarians. Also administered in humans as a way to induce anesthesia, ketamine is noted for a distinct side effect, causing it to be labeled a "dissociative anesthetic." Patients often described an intense out-of-body reaction, when the body feels separated from the mind.

Initially, ketamine was made popular in the 1950s because of its psychedelic effect in which it mimicked phencyclidine, or PCP, but was less likely to cause severe hallucinations and seizures. Used on soldiers during the Vietnam War, it was discontinued due to the intense out-of-body reaction. Its mechanism of action mimics that of PCP but does not suppress breathing, which is why it is still used in humans, and its effect on pain receptors makes ketamine a good analgesic. However, ketamine can affect memory. Also, a person's thoughts can be skewed to the point where they simulate that of a paranoid schizophrenic, and some claim near-death experiences.

Ketamine comes in liquid form that, when heated, allows the saline to be emitted, leaving behind a fine crystalline powder that can be snorted. Ketamine has also been used in conjunction with other drugs and is often mixed with marijuana or ecstasy. Compulsive use is common among those who enjoy its psychedelic effects, especially because the hallucinations or out-of-body experiences only last from a few hours to no more than a day. Ketamine in large quantities can induce a severe form of a dissociated state, in which the user feels disconnected from his own sense of self. Reality as he knows it disappears, and he enters into another world that is indescribable by most. This state is commonly referred to as a "K-hole." The user can experience this other world while remaining semiconscious. Hallucinations may seem all too real and a compelling sense that correlations between the outside world and their own are reinforced. Although most users forget these experiences after coming out of their K-hole, the process can be slow and frightening. Reintegration into the real world can be confusing, and some report a conspiratorial or paranoid residual effect. Often the chronic user will repeatedly try to draw comparisons and look for similarities in the real world as a way to validate his conspiracy theories.

Ketamine is not as addictive as heroin or crystal, yet psychological dependence is common for chronic users. There are no known fatalities associated with ketamine alone, although in combination with other drugs it can be deadly. Older gay men, who have been active partygoers in the past, describe early memory loss, especially of names, even before the age of forty-five. Prolonged use of ketamine, MDMA, or any drug that affects the nervous system can reduce serotonin levels or damage neurons. Studies suggest that SSRIs can actually restore essential neurotransmitters and replenish the reservoir of serotonin.

COCAINE

Cocaine is one of the most glamorized recreational drugs ever. Its mass appeal as a drug for the jet set and the elite became more mainstream in the 1970s because of its association with disco music and dance clubs. Interestingly, cocaine was the original ingredient for the soft drink Coca Cola, but was removed in 1906. Often referred to as "coke," "Chrissy," or "Shirl" on the street, cocaine is a favorite among gay men.

Derived from the coca plant, cocaine is a crystalline powder. Its other forms include "crack," an impure form of freebase that comes in larger rocks as opposed to a fine powder. Cocaine acts as a central nervous system stimulant so that users experience increased energy, euphoria, and loss of appetite. As a result of its nervous system effects, cocaine can be psychologically and physiologically addictive. Despite being illegal worldwide, cocaine use remains pervasive.

The process by which cocaine is produced involves macerating coca leaves with water treated with an acidic solvent like that found in kerosene. The powder is usually then snorted or inhaled. The freebase form does not include the acidic solvent and so is smoked or injected, which is called "slamming." This produces an almost instantaneous rush because it is immediately absorbed in the blood; however, the effects do not last as long as with snorting. Freebase cocaine is made with ether that has to dry off before it is smoked; otherwise it is extremely flammable. In order to get around this, manufacturers began to omit the ether, and this produced an impure form of freebase called "crack" because when it was heated it produced a cracking sound.

Cocaine acts on the brain by inhibiting dopamine reuptake so that the brain is flooded with dopamine. This neurotransmitter acts to elevate mood and increase energy usually within minutes after inhalation and lasting for a few hours or more. Chronic use can lead to decreased levels of normal dopamine signaling so that once a person stops using cocaine, he will experience depression and craving. Also, cocaine works on norepinephrine and serotonin, which affect mood. Long-term use has been associated with severe fluctuations in mood, irritability, weight loss, and paranoia, especially with crack cocaine. Binging can mimic symptoms of schizophrenia, with hallucinations that include the sensation (called formication) that bugs are crawling under your skin.

Sexual desire is grossly exaggerated with cocaine use; however, since the mechanism of action of cocaine is to constrict blood vessels, the penis is unable to engorge with blood. Men may experience erectile dysfunction or impotence as a result. Cocaine users have to rely heavily on prescription erectile dysfunction medication to regain their erections. Nicotine in cigarettes also increases dopamine release so that combining the two produces a heightened sense of euphoria. Many cocaine users also combine their use with alcohol, which helps to offset the agitation or anxiety that can ensue after consuming large quantities. Mixing cocaine with alcohol can result in a common and vicious cycle whereby the user takes more cocaine to overcome the sedating effect of the alcohol and then has to consume more alcohol to fight the agitation. Death in association with cocaine is usually cardiac in nature. Cocaine users are seven times more likely to suffer a heart attack than those who do not use cocaine, and it is estimated that 15 percent of all those who try cocaine will become addicted. Excessive use of cocaine can result in an increased heart rate, elevated blood pressure, and spasms of the coronary arteries, which can all result in a heart attack.

After binging, cocaine users will experience a "crash," which can result in depression, anxiety, and lethargy. Experienced users will try to alleviate these symptoms by smoking pot or using benzodiazepines like Valium and Xanax. Chronic users may experience wild hallucinations, paranoid delusions, and severe muscle twitching. One of the major complications with cocaine is tolerance, which develops over time, and so users must consume higher doses of cocaine in order to sustain the same high. Cocaine can lead to both a physical and a psychological addiction, and a period of readjustment is required once the drug is no longer being taken. Withdrawal symptoms vary in length and severity depending on the length and frequency of use. Symptoms include:

> *agitation*
> *depression*
> *intense cravings*
> *extreme fatigue*
> *anxiety*
> *angry or violent outbursts*
> *decreased motivation*
> *nausea or vomiting*
> *irritability*

> *muscle pain*
> *disturbed sleep patterns*

Chronic inhalation can destroy the sensitive mucous membranes that line the nostrils, and bleeding can occur. Also, the septum that separates the two nasal cavities can erode, leaving a hole. When this happens patients are prone to chronic runny noses and sinusitis. Josh was a chronic cocaine user who developed a nasal septum perforation or an actual hole in his nose due to repeated sniffing. A shield had to be surgically implanted over the hole to aid his breathing and prevent infection. Another common issue with chronic cocaine use is teeth grinding, or bruxism. This strips the enamel and can lead to gingivitis and bleeding.

Cocaine addiction is fairly common, and despite the relative ease of getting patients through the initial craving period once they have stopped, the main issue is controlling the psychological addiction. Benzodiazepines are prescribed to control anxiety and to help with insomnia; however, these drugs are highly addictive. Using behavioral modification, traditional therapy, and twelve-step programs, patients can learn how to live without cocaine. There currently is a class of drugs called selective serotonin-norepinephrine reuptake inhibitors (SNRIs) that are prescribed to treat the withdrawal symptoms that occur once cocaine is discontinued.

CRYSTAL

Methamphetamine, commonly known as Tina, crystal, speed, meth, or ice, is made in illegal underground meth laboratories predominantly in Mexico but also in isolated rural areas in the United States, where the noxious odors won't alert neighbors. Currently, crystal is made from pseudoephedrine, an ingredient found in over-the-counter decongestants like Sudafed. In 2006, federal law restricted the amount of pseudoephedrine a person can buy in a given time period, and has forced pharmacists to store these products behind the counter.

Various recipes to produce crystal call for using ingredients like lithium from rechargeable batteries, mercuric acid, aluminum foil, anhydrous ammonia, which is found in fertilizer, methanol, and muriatic acid. The ingredients are extremely flammable and small meth labs nationwide have reportedly blown up. Also, the makers of meth must endure the highly noxious and poisonous fumes for extended periods of time, which can have debilitating and irrevocable psychological and neurological effects. Meth is dangerous not only to the user but to the rest of society as well. It is estimated that for every pound of meth produced, five to seven pounds of toxic waste is produced.

Methamphetamine was first produced in Japan in the late 1900s and used during World War II to help kamikaze pilots stay awake in order to fly their missions. The Germans also used methamphetamine during the war to maximize their fighting efforts. It has even been suggested that Adolph Hitler took methamphetamine daily. Prior to his death, Hitler showed signs of Parkinson's disease, but one theory is that his movement disorders were a consequence of his crystal use.

Methamphetamine hydrochloride produced as clear, chunky crystals releases high levels of the neurotransmitter dopamine, which stimulates brain cells, enhancing mood and activity. Like cocaine, meth also blocks the re-uptake of dopamine so that the brain is flooded with the neurotransmitter. Crystal also appears to have a neurotoxic effect, damaging brain cells that contain dopamine and serotonin. Over time, methamphetamine appears to reduce levels of dopamine, which can result in symptoms like those of Parkinson's disease, a severe movement disorder. The interesting thing is that unlike cocaine, which has a similar mechanism of action, methamphetamine induces a longer lasting "high," allowing users to stay up for 24 hours and more.

Users usually grind down large chunks into a fine powder and snort it. Immediately, the methamphetamine user experiences an intense sensation, described as euphoric, that lasts several minutes. In addition to the euphoria, users experience an extreme sense of wakefulness and sexual arousal—all of which can lead to addiction. Over time, the meth user requires more and more crystal and must increase the frequency of his use in order to sustain the high. In cases where meth users want to get high quickly, some have resorted to smoking crystal. With smoking, meth users experience an immediate "flash" or "rush" that is more intense than when it is inhaled. Smoking crystal delivers more methamphetamine to the lungs than snorting. Once the crystal enters the lungs, delivery to the brain is expedited. As with cocaine, some users advance to injecting crystal intravenously, or "slamming." Problems associated with smoking crystal or coke include damaging the nasal mucosa and burning your lips. Injecting crystal or coke can put you at risk for developing skin infections and abscesses. Sharing needles leaves you open to contracting hepatitis B, C, and HIV. The cycle of addiction is dependant on the need to maintain the high and to ward off the impending crash, which comes on just as quickly as the high.

Powerful dopaminergic-enhancing drugs like cocaine and crystal have such a high addiction potential because they target the brain-reward center. Stimulating this center causes the brain to want to repeat this behavior. Dr. Steven Lee, who wrote *Overcoming Crystal Meth Addiction*, brilliantly describes how vigorously crystal affects the brain-reward center. Once it has been activated, the brain signals your behavior to do more crystal as a reward. Crystal also destroys brain cells that would normally produce signals telling you not to use crystal. Even as users spiral downward into addiction, many find that they cannot resist because these signals have been obliterated. That is why even when users stop taking crystal for brief periods of time, they can still have intense cravings with just the mere mention or thought of doing meth.

The crystal epidemic has tremendously affected the gay community, especially with the explosion of the circuit party phenomenon. Gay men needed a better alternative to cocaine in order to stay up for extended periods of time. Mixing meth with other party drugs like MDMA, ketamine, and GHB, users had to experiment to find a delicate balance between amazing highs or disastrous consequences. It has been estimated that 20 to 30 percent of all gay men have tried methamphetamine. This statistic will probably increase over the next several years. It is also estimated that over one third of all HIV-positive gay men in the United States have tried crystal. The rise in the number of meth users coincides with HIV seroconversion because of the practice of unprotected sex. Internet chat sites that boast PNP ("party and play") have also created a surge of gay men engaging in drug use and unprotected sex. Some users have resorted to inserting meth crystals in their anus, "the booty bump." This concept is twofold: The rectal mucosa, which has a rich blood supply, absorbs meth readily, while it also acts to constrict blood vessels and nerve endings in the rectum so that intercourse is less painful. This allows bottoms to enjoy prolonged, harder anal intercourse, sometimes with multiple partners. The consequence of the booty bump is that the corrosive ingredients of crystal meth can damage the fragile rectal mucosa and subsequently cause it to tear and bleed. Once this happens, it acts as a vector to infection like STDs and especially HIV.

The number of gay men who report having used crystal is staggering. Even though the San Francisco Department of Health recently announced that crystal use had decreased in the past three years, some clinicians still consider crystal a major health concern. "The numbers are changing," said Dr. Lee. "And it's hard to keep track. Certainly there has been a considerable amount of education in the gay community about the effects of crystal. The fact is that crystal use is increasing among New York City, gay, African-American and Hispanic men, where gay-directed education, outreach, and treatment services are lacking. Worldwide, meth use is growing, and with the exception of marijuana, it is the most widely used illegal drug in the world—30 million meth users compared to 15 million cocaine users and 10 million heroin users. This is more than cocaine and heroin combined."

Crystal produces central nervous system effects like wakefulness, euphoria, decreased appetite, and sexual arousal that are very desirable among gay men who use it for circuit events and sex parties, but there are those men who use it daily as what Dr. Lee calls "the eye opener." Other less desirable effects include extreme irritability, anxiety, paranoia, insomnia, tremors, and aggressive behavior. Despite the increase in libido, meth users develop erectile dysfunction as a result of chronic use. Once meth users transition into addicts, the high they experience gets replaced by hallucinations after prolonged use. A common one is the belief that bugs are crawling under the skin. The street term is *crank bug*. Teeth grinding, or bruxism, is also common, with the possible development of tooth decay and gingivitis aptly described as, "meth mouth." Hyperthermia and convulsions have been the cause of death in certain cases as well as irreversible damage to blood vessels in the brain, causing stroke. Other effects of methamphetamine include respiratory problems (especially when meth is smoked), irregular or increased heart rate, and extreme anorexia. There are numerous documented cases of meth users who have died from cardiovascular collapse, arrhythmia, and myocardial infarction.

Recognizing one's own addiction to crystal meth is the biggest step in beating it, but how do you know if you are an addict? Dr. Lee states that as with any drug, addiction is a loss of control. Signs that suggest you have a problem include:

> *An increase in drug use*
> *Feelings of guilt and depression*
> *Developing drug-related health problems*
> *Increasing the frequency of drug use*
> *Loss of job, friends, and family*

Unlike as for alcohol and heroin, there is no FDA-approved medication for the treatment of methamphetamine withdrawal. First and foremost, the consensus among clinicians is that the best way to quit is to stop using it completely. For the chronic user this is easier said then done. Besides the impending crash and subsequent depression, crystal users must battle the brain-reward system that has been reprogrammed to want crystal. The

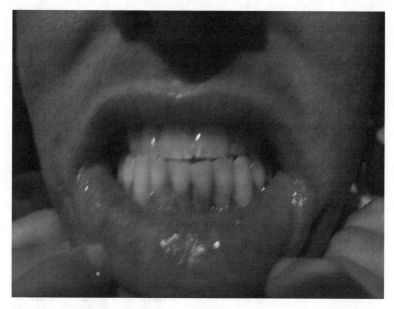

"Meth Mouth," Gums receding
Note the ill health of the gums (gingivitus) and tooth decay from
"bruxism," or grinding of the teeth, caused by repeated use of
crystal methamphetamine, a popular recreational drug of many gay
men. Photos by the author.

process of recovery is complicated and many successful
gay men have found that Crystal Meth Anonymous
(CMA) is a great outlet for them to express their fears
and their struggles. There are several prescription drugs
that can be utilized in conjunction with your health-care
provider to deal with the strong cravings or symptoms
associated with the "crash" and erratic sleep habits. Medications such as Wellbutrin (bupropion) or amantadine
can increase dopamine levels. These drugs have been
shown to be helpful for recovering meth users by restor-
ing energy and improving mood. Also these dopaminergic medications have also been shown to protect the
brain from damage caused by meth. It is recommended

that benzodiazepines (Ativan, Xanax, or Klonopin), be avoided. Although these drugs can effectively treat anxiety and help with sleep, they are highly addicting. Also, the use of Provigil (modafinil) has been found to increase energy and attention, which is essential for recovery. Case reports also indicate that since modafinil has less dopaminergic activity, it is less addictive and helps to balance brain chemistry. Regardless of individual case reports by some doctors, use of these medications is based on a prescriber's experience. It is imperative that addicts find an addiction specialist. Medications used to treat addiction can have unfortunate side effects that need to be monitored.

GHB (GAMMA-HYDROXYBUTYRATE)

GHB, or G, liquid ecstasy, and Gina, is a central nervous system depressant. As a naturally occurring substance that is a precursor to the neurotransmitter that regulates wakefulness, the drug form comes in a salt using either sodium or potassium. Synthesized in the early 1960s, GHB has a variety of effects on the body. Moderate doses cause euphoria, sexual enhancement, and elevated mood. Originally developed as an anesthetic, GHB had too many unwarranted side effects. At higher doses, it induces sleep to such extremes that it mimics coma.

In the United States, GHB was marketed to bodybuilders and sold in health food stores as a growth hormone stimulant to increase lean muscle. GHB came into notoriety as the date rape drug because the liquid form could be put into an unsuspecting person's drink, causing dizziness, nausea, decreased breathing, and unconsciousness. The effects of GHB can last from one to three hours and even longer if ingested with alcohol. In 1990, it was taken off the shelves of health food stores and the FDA halted distribution.

As a recreational drug, GHB became very popular among gay men who used it in low doses to produce an intense sense of euphoria and increased libido. Commonly purchased off the Internet and brewed at home, GHB is dissolved in water, carbonated sodas, and energy drinks, and then ingested. The danger with GHB lies in its formulation and how much is required to achieve the desired high. Since the salt concentration of the liquid mixture can have varying concentrations, the actual dose of GHB may be unknown. This can make estimating the amount of GHB consumed difficult to judge accurately. Compounding this is the fact that the slope to intoxication is very steep. Much like alcohol, once intoxication begins to take effect, the user may have already ingested more then enough GHB. The cumulative effect can be deadly.

A GHB overdose can result in seizures, vomiting, unconsciousness, and respiratory depression. Death is associated with GHB most often when it is mixed with other neurological depressants like alcohol or drugs like benzodiazepines or ketamine. Overdose is usually noted about thirty to sixty minutes after ingestion. The progression of a GHB overdose begins as the users starts to look very high—overly energetic, sweating profusely, eyes bulging. Then, as the cumulative effect of the GHB sets in, the user will have intermittent loss of motor function—knees buckle, eyes droop—and will appear as if he is nodding off. In the early stages, the user will be able to regain consciousness, as the effects of GHB are cyclical. Many try to combat the effect by drinking caffeinated beverages and snorting crystal methamphetamine; however, once a user loses consciousness, arousal will only be obtained after the GHB has worn off.

Chronic users usually maintain a consistency with their GHB, using only the same batch that they have and never mixing it with someone else's. GHB is distributed in capfuls and sold in glass vials. The caustic ingredients of the GHB salt can be very harmful. Ingestion has been known to cause nausea, vomiting, and stomach ulceration. Once a couple told me that after mixing GHB, they left a plastic cupful on their dresser before going out for the evening. When they returned it had eaten through the plastic cup and dissolved the paint off the furniture. This is understandable because the precursor to GHB can be made from paint stripper or varnish thinner.

GHB overdoses require immediate medical attention because users can stop breathing and their heart rate can diminish substantially to produce heart failure. Ingenious users attempt to reverse the sedating affects of GHB by combining it with stimulants like crystal. This is not effective in the unconscious patient. Most cases of GHB overdose require monitoring for breathing and heart rate as the user sleeps off the effects of GHB. Other common and worrisome effects include seizures and vomiting, which requires airway protection so that the person does not asphyxiate. Many men who have overdosed wake up in an ICU attached to a respirator; however, this may not deter them from using GHB again.

It goes without saying that among gay male partygoers, GHB combined with crystal is a perfect marriage of recreational drugs. One provides the user with a vo-

WHILE WORKING on Fire Island one summer, I was made aware of an overdose in which a young man became unconscious after ingesting too much GHB. His housemates said he became stuporous while sitting in the hot tub. The heat from the water acted to accelerate his loss of consciousness. Then instead of calling an ambulance, his friends began to insert cocaine in his rectum in order to resuscitate him. Needless to say, he died. The point is that if you are in a situation where someone appears to be in danger do not attempt to revive him unless you know what you are doing. Playing doctor or alchemist could jeopardize a life and ruin yours.

racious sexual appetite, while the other supplies the superhuman stamina to satiate it. Needless to say, GHB can be addicting both physically and psychologically, and withdrawal can result in insomnia, restlessness, anxiety, muscle aches, depression, and loss of appetite.

Treatment for men who seek help for GHB addiction follows a similar plan as for most other recreational drugs. The consensus among clinicians is to quit cold turkey. Drug rehabilitation is a multifaceted, long-term process. Detoxification is the first step, but detoxification alone will not change a user's habits. Recovery involves the assistance from addiction professionals. In order for a successful recovery, treatment must provide addicts with new tools to deal with present situations and problems that can arise. Treating patients with antidepressants will assist the recovery process, but most clinicians agree that treating the underlying issue is the most important factor in recovery. In many cases, treating users with a short course of antidepressants is essential to restore brain chemistry. These medications also provide relief from the stress of withdrawal and should be used in conjunction with psychotherapy and behavioral modification therapy.

MARIJUANA

Marijuana is the most commonly used illegal drug in the United States. The National Institute on Drug Abuse published findings in 2004 that 14.6 million Americans ages twelve and older used marijuana at least once in the month prior to being surveyed. About six thousand people a day used marijuana in 2004. Currently, it is estimated that more than 20 percent of Americans use marijuana.

Derived from the hemp plant, *Cannabis sativa,* a dried mixture of flowers, stems, seeds, and leaves is usually smoked as a cigarette called a joint or in a pipe or bong. Marijuana is sometimes mixed with food, the most familiar being pot brownies, or blended into brews such as teas.

The countless street terms for marijuana include pot, herb, weed, grass, ganja, and hash. The main active ingredient in marijuana is THC (delta-9-tetrahydrocannabinol), which binds to protein receptors in the brain. Once in place, THC initiates a series of cellular reactions that ultimately leads to the high. Smoking marijuana quickly allows THC to be absorbed by the lungs and enter the bloodstream where it passes to other organs. In the brain, there are cannabinoid receptors that influence pleasure, memory, thought, concentration, sensory and time perception, and coordinated movement.

The short-term effects of marijuana can include problems with memory and learning; distorted perception; difficulty in thinking and problem-solving; loss of coordination; and increased heart rate. The DSM suggested that chronic, heavy use of marijuana caused Amotivational syndrome, characterized by a person's unwillingness to work, attend school, or perform activities that required prolonged periods of attention. Other researchers have refuted this association with chronic marijuana use. Results from research performed at the University of Pittsburgh School of Medicine did not indicate any overall pattern of excess psychopathology. Their findings suggested that heavy marijuana use may be related to a preexisting, underlying depression and that it caused impaired motivation.

In addition to these cognitive impairments, people who smoke marijuana are more likely to suffer from respiratory illnesses, although a major confounding factor is that many users also admitted to alcohol and tobacco use. The National Institute on Drug Abuse findings, along with other research studies, indicate that those who smoke marijuana regularly may have many of the same respiratory problems that tobacco smokers do, such as cough and phlegm production, more frequent acute chest illness, a heightened risk of lung infections, and a greater tendency toward obstructed airway disease. Smoking marijuana possibly increases the likelihood of developing cancer of the head, neck, and lungs. Marijuana smoke contains 50 to 70 percent more carcinogenic hydrocarbons than tobacco smoke. Since most marijuana users inhale more deeply and hold their breath longer than tobacco smokers do, their risk of exposing their lungs to carcinogenic smoke is greater. Smoking cannabis contains all the toxic constituents of smoke—except nicotine—including irritants, tumor initiators, carbon monoxide, and carcinogens.

Research has also suggested that marijuana affects blood pressure, heart rate, and the oxygen-carrying capacity of blood. One study even suggested that the risk for heart attack quadruples in the first hour after smoking pot.

It has also been suggested that THC impairs the body's immune response. This is a critical issue for gay men with HIV. The inability to fight infection puts users at a higher risk for developing infection. Interestingly, medical cannabis effectively treats nausea and has been used in cancer patients undergoing chemotherapy as well as HIV patients on antiretrovirals. The appetite-stimulating effect of medical cannabis, commonly referred to as "the munchies," also promotes weight gain in these two patient groups. Under U.S. law, cannabis is registered as a Schedule I drug, while the prescription drug dronabinol, brand name Marinol, is an oral formulation listed as Schedule III, despite the fact that they have the same active ingredient.

Since marijuana is strongly absorbed by fatty tissues in various organs of the body, THC can usually be detected in urine for several days after marijuana has been smoked. If marijuana is used heavily, traces of THC may be detected in urine for several weeks. This is a major concern for users who are asked to undergo drug testing.

Long-term use has also been associated with addiction. Drug craving and withdrawal symptoms are common and make it even harder for chronic users to stop. Rebound irritability, insomnia, and anxiety are common symptoms.

Cognitive-behavioral therapy has been found to benefit chronic marijuana users. One study of adult users found comparable benefits from cognitive-behavioral group treatment and individual treatment that included motivational interviewing and advice on ways to reduce marijuana use. Participants were mostly men in their early thirties who had smoked marijuana daily for more than ten years. By increasing awareness of what triggers their marijuana abuse, both treatments sought to help users devise avoidance strategies. Abuse, dependence symptoms, and psychosocial problems decreased for at least a year following both treatments; about 30 percent of former users were still abstinent during the last three-month follow-up period.

AMYL NITRITE (POPPERS)

Amyl nitrite acts by dilating blood vessels and lowering blood pressure. It is used for treatment of heart disease, especially angina, and for cyanide poisoning. Recreationally, amyl nitrite is inhaled as "poppers," and provides a temporary high due to its action on nitric oxide. Poppers come as a liquid in glass vials, which, when opened, release a distinct odor that is inhaled. The effects are almost immediate but last only a few minutes. Physical effects include a decrease in blood pressure, headache, flushing of the skin, increase in pulse rate, and light-headedness.

Popularized in the 1970s by gay men in dance bars, handkerchiefs soaked with amyl nitrite were passed around. The desired effect was to provide an instantaneous high along with a heightened sense of sexual arousal. In addition to the predominant effects of amyl nitrite, there is relaxation of involuntary muscles, especially the anal sphincter. Gay men utilize this as an aid to anal intercourse.

Most clinicians agree that amyl nitrite is not recommended as a sexual aid. In addition to sudden death, other dangerous side effects include irregular heart rates, heart failure, respiratory depression, neurological dysfunction, and nasal mucosa and skin irritation following acute exposure. Ira used poppers routinely but dropped the bottle on his partner's face after becoming severely lightheaded. His partner sustained burns to his cheek, nose, and left ear resulting in a temporary loss of hearing.

Nitrite inhalation has also been implicated in immune system depression. This has caused some HIV providers to suspect that use of poppers might also facilitate viral replication. These studies have helped clarify the association between nitrite inhalant use, immune dysfunction, and evolving patterns of HIV. For example, KS is one of the manifestations of AIDS to have shown a decrease since 1981, and this has coincided with the decrease in the use of nitrite inhalants by homosexual men.

More important is that with the variety of erectile dysfunction medications, the use of "poppers" or any other form of nitrites is strongly prohibited due to the cumulative effect on lowering blood pressure. The result can be prolonged loss of consciousness and even death.

SMOKING AND ALCOHOL

So much attention in the gay community has been focused on recreational drugs, especially crystal methamphetamine addiction, but the truth is that alcohol and nicotine are more predominant. The CDC reports that in the United States over 400,000 deaths annually are attributed to tobacco, while over 100,000 are due to alcohol-related deaths

Alcohol addiction can cause severe liver damage, often resulting in organ failure and death. For people who are unable to stop drinking on their own, alcohol rehabilitation may be the only way to quit this potentially fatal habit. Nicotine, one of the most addictive drugs on the market, is known to cause lung cancer and emphysema. Currently, there are FDA-approved medications on the market to combat these highly addictive problems.

Tips on How to Identify an Addict

No one sets out to become dependent on drugs or alcohol. Usually the course of events leading up to addiction involves overcoming stresses or problems in daily life. Addiction tends to mask deeper emotional or psychological problems that the individual is unable to cope with. But what usually begins as escapism or a way to "feel better" only makes things worse. The important thing to remember is that addicts need professional help, and until they enter a rehabilitation program, their problems will likely worsen over time. Physical changes to look for include:

> *Sudden weight loss*
> *Extreme mood swings*
> *Changes in sleep patterns*
> *Red, watery eyes*
> *Dilated or constricted pupils*
> *Depression*
> *Cold, sweaty palms*
> *Persistent runny nose*
> *Tremors or shakes*
> *Puffiness in the face or around the eyes, with pale or reddened skin*

In addition to these physical symptoms, note any of the following behavioral changes:

> *Change in friends*
> *Secretive behavior*
> *Paranoia and defensiveness*
> *Forgetfulness and lying*
> *Problems at work and increased absenteeism*
> *Lack of personal hygiene*
> *Violent or bizarre behavior*
> *Loss of interest in family and friends*
> *Moodiness, nervousness, and irritability*
> *Hyperactivity*

Tips on Staying Sober

> *Avoid hanging around with friends who continue to take drugs.*
> *Avoid situations and events where you know drugs or alcohol will be available.*
> *Try to keep your free time occupied with productive activities.*

> *Continue attending individual and group therapy sessions like Crystal Meth Anonymous or Alcoholics Anonymous on a regular basis.*
> *Volunteer your time at a drug rehabilitation centers in order to share your experiences with other recovering addicts.*

CHAPTER 13

The Gay Body Beautiful

AN OBSESSION with one's appearance is a corner-stone of gay culture. The desire to look good and a willingness to improve on your general appearance can be healthy concerns, especially when they are supported by good nutrition and exercise. However, for some, the fixation on perfection can be debilitating, and having an unhealthy preoccupation with your body might even suggest low self-esteem. This was supported in a 2005 report published in the *Journal of Consulting and Clinical Psychology,* which stated that some gay men have a fixation with their body image as a response to concerns over internalized homophobia, social prejudice, and a desire to conform to heterosexual norms. Other similar reports indicate that dissatisfaction with one's looks is more predominant in gay men than their heterosexual counterparts. This, despite the rising popularity of metrosexuals, a term coined by Mark Simpson in his article, "The Independent," which glorified the growing number of men, said to be heterosexual, who share a strong aesthetic sense.

The metrosexual is defined as a man who deeply cares about his outward appearance and how it pertains to his lifestyle. The reality, unfortunately, is that many homosexuals have such an irrational preoccupation with their appearance that it borders on dimorphism. Body dysmorphic disorder (BDD) is an unhealthy—and highly critical—obsession with one's appearance that interferes with daily life. It has been further suggested that BDD is directly related to an alarming number of gay men who suffer from suicidal thoughts, depression, anxiety, and substance abuse.

One response to these old, effeminate stereotypes has been to refute them, by presenting an idealized masculine appearance. This was done in order to rebuke the misconception that all gay men are feminine. Unfortunately for some, this argument has produced a number of men who have become fixated with the notion that being muscular is synonymous with being masculine. The rationale is that big men are "real men." True, some gay men become bodybuilders or muscle men because they are very attracted to this form of masculinity and want to be desired. Because of this growing phenomenon is another, in which gay men refer to themselves as "straight acting," in order to disguise their deep-rooted feelings of insecurity. This theme promotes a new wave of gay men—those who are not effeminate and can "pass" for straight.

The idea of "passing" as straight became even more pronounced once the peak of the AIDS epidemic had passed. Being identified as gay posed the new risk of

THE PRESSURE to conform within gay society is so great that for the dysmorphic man it may result in physical changes that border on grotesque. When I first ventured into a gay gym in 1997, I was astounded by all the overinflated men who reminded me of old illustrations of "the missing link." Interestingly, I felt a strong sexual response to these men. Perhaps it was because I grew up with few gay role models and I did not identify with such queer celebrities as Paul Lynde in the center square, or Charles Nelson Reilly on *The Match Game.* Their silly affectations drove me deeper into my closeted existence. Now I realize how truly wonderful they really were, but back then the implication that these icons represented what being gay was all about truly frightened me. Certainly, there was a lack of masculine gay men in the media. So to see gay muscle men at the gym for the first time was a shocking revelation.

being identified as having AIDS. This very epidemic also redefined the gay body image as lipodystrophy, a direct consequence of AIDS and HIV medication. Lipodystrophy syndrome is defined as visible body changes in which fat gets redistributed so that it accumulates on the back of the neck, dubbed by HIV-positive gay men as "buffalo hump," or around the midsection, also known as "Crix belly," after the protease inhibitor Crixivan. Other upsetting changes called lipoatrophy involve fat loss in the cheeks and temples, which result in a gaunt appearance named "AIDS face" by some men. Other signs of severe fat loss are also seen in the arms and legs, with disturbing effects resulting in what appears as excessively ripped muscles and prominent cablelike veins. Lipodystrophy has become a major cause for alarm for men who worry about looking like they have HIV.

"I can deal with the virus," said Matthew, a recent seroconverter. "I just don't want to look like I'm sick!"

Matthew is not alone, and his fear is shared by many men, especially those with longstanding HIV. Even after surviving the worst of the epidemic, the potentially disfiguring effects of HIV are all too real. They can be seen every day in the faces and bodies of HIV infected people who feel as if they wear these changes like a scarlet letter.

"I used to love the summer," said Tom, who has been struggling with lipodystrophy for ten years. "When I go to the beach now, I feel like everyone is staring at me." Tom has resorted to wearing baseball caps to distract attention from his hollowed cheeks and adamantly refuses to wear short pants.

At the onset of this new turn of events, clinicians scrambled to figure out what was causing lipodystrophy. Was it HIV or something else entirely?

Studies show that lipodystrophy syndrome is linked to changes at the cellular level. That means that the virus itself, over time, can cause changes leading to insulin resistance and mitochondrial toxicity, which results in both fat loss and redistribution. Interestingly, certain antiretrovirals used to treat HIV can also cause these changes. Older drugs, especially ones in the class known as protease inhibitors, have been linked to lipodystrophy, as have some nucleoside analogs, like Zerit (stavudine), Videx (didanosine), and AZT (retrovir). It is estimated that roughly 80 percent of HIV positive men on cocktails containing one or more of these medications has lipodystrophy. Risk also increases with older age, longer lengths of treatment, and poorer immune systems.

Even as clinicians raced to change some HIV cocktails, treatment focused on the use of anabolic steroids, testosterone replacement, and growth hormone. As a result, the HIV body image was distorted even further for some men. These medications designed to treat the devastating affects of HIV wasting had altered the physical appearance of the HIV positive male. Instead of seeing malnourished-looking bodies, these men became overly muscular and grotesque.

Nevertheless, the abuse potential for steroids grew exponentially, and as a result they have become incorporated into mainstream gay culture as a way to achieve the perfect body. The concern with steroid abuse is something that many clinicians find perplexing, even as the long-term effects became apparent. Gay men still found ways to get steroids, and the phenomenon of getting bigger has become a global issue. The masculinization of homosexuals is based on an inherent need for acceptance. The fact is that some gay men, no matter how big they get, will never feel good about themselves.

WILLIAM, A six-foot-tall, 325-pound male, came to my office for a complete physical after being referred by his psychiatrist. With his shaved head and big blue eyes, he looked like the Thing from the Fantastic Four. After the initial interview, I realized that this beast of a man was as sweet and soft-spoken as a lamb. He had been undergoing intensive therapy for steroid abuse. William had been using a combination of high-dose anabolics and male hormones for the past five years. The use of these steroids was a direct result of physical abuse he suffered as a child for being gay. His response was retaliation for this ridicule, and so he transformed himself into a monster. This was the most severe form of dysmorphism I had ever witnessed. Unfortunately, William's exterior was the complete antithesis of his inner self, which was still quite wounded and insecure. Over the course of a year, William had attempted suicide, continued to abuse steroids, and remained clinically depressed. His story, although extreme, is one that touches on all the facets of the gay body image.

Anabolic steroids have fueled the fires of our body-conscious community. They have even pushed some men into experimenting with different steroid combinations and utilizing black market sources because steroids are illegal in the United States for cosmetic purposes. Physically, steroids build up lean body mass, increase sex drive, and improve strength. Psychologically, they provide a false sense of security by instilling a feeling of vitality and sexuality in users. The flip side is serious bouts of aggression, depression, and hostility.

The use of steroids and certain supplements can also adversely affect your health due to their addiction potential. In treating HIV wasting, there are protocols on how to administer steroids for specific periods of time. Cycling refers to this idea of utilizing steroids for a specific period and then coming off them in order for your body to adjust to the changes. While administering a cycle of steroids, patients are monitored regularly for abnormalities in their serum chemistries and liver function. Many gay men who use steroids educate themselves with information from the same unreliable sources they have procured them from. Buying illegal steroids from outside the United States also brings up the issue of quality. Since there are no government agencies monitoring these illegal sources, products have inconsistent outcomes due to impurities. There are documented cases of liver failure, heart problems, and blood pressure issues associated with anabolic steroids. Although all patients should be warned against their use, the topic should be discussed openly with a doctor so that one can be educated about the risks associated with their use.

The use of anabolic steroids is dangerous, especially for extended periods without a break. The androgenic effects of anabolics and testosterone can cause testicles to shrivel up because of the negative feedback inhibition. When men self-administer exogenous testosterone, this sends a message to the brain to stop their testicles from producing testosterone. Usually once the exogenous steroid has been discontinued, the testicles resume production of testosterone, but this can take months or more. During that time, men experience extreme fatigue, depression, and loss of libido. Some men, especially those who abuse steroids for prolonged periods of time, never regain their testicular function and thrust themselves into early andropause. These cases require permanent testosterone replacement therapy. (If you are going to use steroids, tell your doctor and remember to cycle off for as long as you have been on.)

Some of the more common side effects that occur as a result of anabolic steroid and testosterone use include:

Acne. A surge in the level of testosterone will make you think you are going through puberty again. Acne, usually on the face and back, is common in men who use high doses of steroids and testosterone or those who cycle too quickly. The severity of the acne is due to the body's inability to adjust to the changes in hormone levels. Usually the acne resolves once the hormone balance has been achieved; otherwise, common acne products, like benzoyl peroxidase wash, will help reduce the spread.

Hair loss. The presence of androgens, testosterone, and its related hormone DHT, cause hair follicles to shrink up and die. The most common form of male pattern baldness is called androgenetic alopecia, which refers to dihydrotestosterone (DHT.) This is formed by the action of the enzyme 5-a reductase on testosterone. When DHT binds to special receptor sites on hair follicles, this causes specific changes associated with balding. In cases where men use high doses of testosterone for cosmetic use, taking Propecia (finasteride) can offset the hair loss due to its inhibition of the enzyme 5-a reductase.

High blood pressure. Certain steroids, like testosterone, nandrolone, and oxymetholone, can raise blood pressure. The mechanism by which this occurs is directly related to water retention and elevated hematocrit. An increased hematocrit means that there are too many red blood cells, or polycythemia. If the number of red blood cells goes up, then the blood becomes thicker. This increase in blood viscosity can also result in blood clots, strokes, and heart attacks. Steroids are also linked to elevated cholesterol, another risk factor for stroke and heart disease. Careful monitoring of all these blood tests is essential to reduce the risk of cardiovascular and neurological diseases.

Gynecomastia. Male breast development is caused by overproduction of estrogen, which occurs when a man is exposed to increased levels of testosterone. Testosterone converts into estrogen, and subsequently the tissue under the areola can develop. This is commonly referred to as "bitch tits." Sometimes the tissue can be quite tender and the nipples can be very sensitive, but not in a good way. To counteract the excess estrogen, some clinicians prescribe anti-estrogens. In severe cases, the tissue has to be removed surgically.

Elevated liver enzymes. The effects of steroids on liver function are controversial; however, most clinicians agree that it is dose dependant. This means that prolonged use of high-dose steroids can potentially lead to liver toxicity, especially if patients are on other medications that are cleared by the liver. Routine liver function tests should be performed to monitor trends, especially for HIV-positive men on antiretroviral medication.

Dealing with steroid abusers is challenging. Getting them to stop involves extensive behavioral modification. Once they have committed to the idea, most men have to contend with a significant amount of weight loss. This is followed by an intense fear that they are "shrinking." Therapy is often necessary to redirect how gay men perceive themselves. In some cases men are put on antidepressants for a short course to get them through the severe depression and lethargy. Also, working through the physical symptoms associated with a low libido can be extremely challenging. Prolonged loss of sex drive can lead some men to resume steroid use. This is because their depressed libido is not simply a case of erectile dysfunction. Consult your doctor for treatment if symptoms after steroid use are prolonged or intolerable. Remember that protracted courses of steroids can cause irreversible damage.

Conversely, the opposite is true for gay men who aspire to look more like fashion models. These men fall into the dangerous world of eating disorders. Harvard researchers reported the results of the first national study of eating disorders in a population of nearly three thousand adults and found that 25 percent of those with anorexia or bulimia and 40 percent of binge eaters were men. Another study estimates that 20 percent of those men are gay. Unlike the female ideal, which tends to focus on a "goal weight," or overall skinniness, men's focus is nearly always on achieving "six-pack" abs. In contrast to the number of female celebrities who have publicly discussed their eating disorders, few well-known men have come forward.

Actor Dennis Quaid has talked openly about his battle with what he calls "manorexia," for which he sought treatment. Other celebrities like actor Billy Bob Thornton and singer Elton John have come forward about their struggles with bulimia. Eating disorders are psychiatric conditions that are associated with a distorted body image, low self-esteem, and feelings of insecurity, which are common themes among gay men.

Bulimia, characterized by binge eating, is especially common among homosexuals. The physical effects include rapid weight loss, dehydration, fatigue, low heart rate, and low blood pressure. Psychologically, men with eating disorders suffer from isolation, depression, suicidal thoughts, and anxiety. After a person binges, they usually develop feelings of embarrassment, guilt, or self-hatred. These feelings force the bulimic into prolonged starvation, self-induced vomiting, and abuse of laxatives and diuretics.

It is not surprising to find that gay men are quite honest about their eating habits. Most readily admit to vomiting, using laxatives, and restrictive dieting in order to lose weight when questioned by their doctor. As with any eating disorder, health-care concerns are paramount. Fluctuations in weight are attributable to heart disease and immune suppression. Warning signs that you might have an eating disorder include:

> *Always counting calories*
> *Feeling unsatisfied with your body*
> *Inducing vomiting and using laxatives*
> *Feeling anxious about food*

Treatment for males involves cognitive therapy to overcome a distorted body image, which is at the core of all eating disorders. Screening patients for depression and substance abuse is also important because the two conditions are often present.

Trying to redirect the focus of the gay body image is a constant battle. Societal strains and the media do so much to propagate the image of a perfect body and a handsome face that getting past this often seems impossible. If you feel you have an eating disorder or are abusing steroids, contact your physician for help. It is vital to know that concerns over body image are not restricted to the young. As we get older and our bodies start to age, there is even more pressure to feel as though we fit in.

In order to combat the battle with age, some gay men have resorted to surgery. Facial enhancement and liposuction have become increasingly popular with gay men, especially the HIV-positive community that has suffered greatly from the effects of lipodystrophy. In fact, it has become a medical necessity for those men suffering from facial wasting. These devastating effects of HIV and HIV treatment have transformed a subgroup of infected men and branded them with a recognizable deformity. Unfortunately, so much of what clinicians know now about lipodystrophy is the result of hindsight. Currently, treatment strategies to combat lipodystrophy consist of drug substitutions, facial fillers, and plastic surgery.

Patients with advanced HIV facial wasting will not benefit from drug substitutions, although switching regimens will decrease the progression of atrophy. By changing their antiretroviral medication, the progression of lipoatrophy will be reduced. Once the damage has been done, however, altering medication will not bring back your face. In 2002, there were few treatments available for facial wasting; all involved injecting various products, called facial fillers, directly into the face. One of the earliest products used was silicone, which is not FDA-approved for facial wasting but is still used, especially on the West Coast, despite its permanent effects. The major concern with silicone is that it has the potential to become encapsulated under the skin where it forms granulomas, an inflammatory growth. These tumorlike lesions can appear many years after the injections. In addition to their disfiguring affect, they can cause serious infections and are difficult to treat.

Currently, the FDA has approved a line of products made from polylactic acid. A commonly used product by the brand name Sculptra has proven to be highly successful. Although temporary, the impressive results can last for up to a year. Most patients require several treatments initially to get the desired effect, with additional treatments scheduled six to twelve months later depending on the patient. Sanofi Aventis, the maker of Sculptra, offers an assistance program to patients with HIV who are unable to pay for the product themselves. To apply, check out their Web site at www.sculptra.com.

There are a variety of other facial fillers. If you are interested, get a recommendation for a good dermatologist or plastic surgeon.

The surgical options for treating lipoatrophy also include the use of facial implants. Submalar or combination malar/submalar implants are used to replace volume loss. The downside is that they can cause an allergic reaction in a small percentage of patients. Other problems associated with implants is that they can migrate from the area in which they were initially set. Serious infection and inflammation can occur at the surgical site and chronic long-term inflammation and infection are possible in up to 3 percent of cases. Options for fat excess include liposuction, especially in the midsection and neck, to remove unwanted fat. Unfortunately, the treatment for lipodystrophy is considered cosmetic and can be expensive. If you are going to make the investment, find a doctor with expertise or one highly recommended by someone you trust.

Looking good has become just as much a status symbol for gay men as driving the right car or owning the perfect New York apartment. "Having a perfect smile is just as important as owning a Rolex," said one patient. The field of cosmetic dentistry has exploded in the last five years. Dr. Avo Samuelian commented that "the technology required to change a person's smile is readily available and revolutionary." "I hated my smile and since my parents didn't believe in braces, I have been self-conscious all my life," said John, a patient. After nine months with the Invisalign, a clear plastic alternative to metal braces, John now has perfect teeth. Likewise, brighter, whiter teeth can also be achieved with various bleaches or the BriteSmile tooth-whitening system. This procedure can lighten your smile in just ninety minutes, although the effects are not long lasting. Still, for some, impatience with braces has led to an influx of men requesting porcelain veneers in order to correct overcrowding and misalignment. To create a veneer, a porcelain covering is sculpted to the individual tooth after it has been reduced. Most veneers last approximately ten to fifteen years.

Dr. David Colbert, a board certified dermatologist, has also noted an increase in men coming into his office for cosmetic procedures. "Botox by far leads the way as the number one procedure because it is easy, fast, and almost painless. I tend to vary the amount injected so that men won't look as if they have had 'work done.' A smooth forehead and no crow's feet have become the new standard for a great-looking face. Practically any forty-something guy can look thirty with a little Botox."

The use of Botox has become a cultural phenomenon

since receiving FDA approval in 2002 for the temporary treatment of moderate to severe frown lines between the brows. Derived from a purified form of botulinum toxin, Botox acts to paralyze certain facial muscles upon injection, to inhibit their actions, and to decrease wrinkling. According to Allergan, the maker of Botox, over three million procedures were performed in 2005 alone. In fact, the American Society for Aesthetic Plastic Surgery ranked Botox Cosmetic as the most popular physician-administered aesthetic procedure in the United States for the fourth year in a row.

Second to Botox are fillers for deep nasolabial lines, of which Perlane and Radiesse are the most commonly used. Dr. Colbert finds that gay men look for a stronger jaw line, which can be achieved by using fat injections, facial filler like Radiesse or Perlane, or implants. Another popular procedure is microliposuction of the submental area, which tightens and sharpens the jaw line. Often men do combination treatments. The triad facial—microdermabrasion, laser toning, and a chemical peeling—is also extremely popular with gay men. This results in smaller pores, tighter skin, and an overall healthy glow. Another growing trend is for lip fillers to achieve a thicker, fuller lip.

Laser beard grooming to remove hair from the upper cheeks and lower neck is easier than shaving daily and results in a clean-cut appearance, even with a little stubble. According to Dr. Colbert, the majority of men who get laser beard sculpturing wish to get rid of the facial hair on their neck. Afterward, most men can go without shaving for three to four days without looking scruffy. Laser beard treatments also alleviate razor burns and annoying cuts, especially for men who have heavy beards and sensitive skin. For most gay men, the staple proce-

Dr. Frank's Tips on Maintaining Healthy Skin and Reducing Wrinkles

1. Avoid the sun if possible. If you are in the sun, protect your eyes with sunglasses and wear sunscreen.
2. Drink plenty of water and get an adequate amount of sleep. Water both hydrates cells and helps them to mobilize toxins out of the body while maintaining nutrients. Lack of sleep produces the hormone cortisol, which breaks down skin cells. Sleeping promotes growth hormone production, which helps retain the skin's elasticity.
4. Eliminate caffeine from your diet. Caffeine dehydrates skin. Consider replacing it with cocoa, which contains high levels of two dietary flavanols—epicatchin and catechin—that make skin feel and look smoother.
5. Moisturize your skin daily. Avoid overwashing your face with soap. Use a cleanser instead and

dure is laser hair removal and shaping of chest hair. "Now there is no reason for unsightly back hair or unibrows," said Dr. Colbert. Laser resurfacing is also used to remove

moisturize to protect skin from wrinkles.

6. Sleep on your back. Sleeping on your stomach and side can etch wrinkles into your face that will not diminish over time.

7. Check out omega-3 fatty acids. Salmon (and other fish) as well as walnuts (and other nuts) are high in this essential fatty acid. Omega-3 helps to maintain cell membranes by keeping harmful toxins out and allowing nutrients to enter cells.

8. Eat lots of fruits and vegetables. Blueberries and carrots are high in antioxidants and target free radicals, which are harmful to the skin.

9. Shave safely. Avoid skin irritation by pressing a warm wash cloth onto your face before shaving in order to soften hair. Never shave a dry face, and for best results shave after showering, preferably with a lotion or gel to keep the skin lubricated. Use a clean razor and shave in the direction of hair growth. Rinse with warm water.

10. Stop smoking. Smoking causes the release of enzymes that break down collagen and elastin.

the top layer of skin. This promotes the skin's natural collagen production, resulting in smoother, less wrinkled skin. Less expensive procedures that remove the top layer of skin to promote natural collagen production are chemical peels, which actually wash away the top layer of skin, and dermabrasion, which employs a crystal to abrade the skin and remove the top layer.

In addition to these various facial-enhancement procedures, many gay men are flocking to their plastic surgeons for more permanent results. Dr. Robert Tornambe is a board-certified plastic surgeon who has also noticed the growing trend of gay men seeking out professional consultations for surgical procedures. "The movement is toward less invasive procedures," said Dr. Tornambe. This means less radical surgery so that the healing time is shorter. "Most gay men want liposuction for their spare tires and love handles. The goal is a more natural, athletic-appearing body. In addition to liposuction, there is a concern with drooping eyes and abnormal breast tissue growth."

The best advice for anyone seeking out a surgical consult is to ensure that the surgeon has performed a sufficient amount of procedures on male patients. For instance, blepharoplasty, or eye lifts, are increasingly popular with gay men, but the results can be disastrous when performed by surgeons who do them primarily on women. "Blepharoplasty is less dramatic on a male patient," said Dr. Tornambe. "The idea is not to give the appearance of having had surgery at all."

Other common procedures Dr. Tornambe performs routinely are ultrasonic liposuction, which uses sound waves to break up fat cells. "This is useful, especially for the midsection and works well for gynecomastia." Also full face lifts are being replaced by the mini facelift, which is a short scar revision. "This procedure is for younger patients aged forty to fifty as a way to 'tighten up things' using smaller incisions and less aggressive remodeling of the underlying muscle. This procedure primarily targets one area, like the neck," he said. The intent is to make an aging face look much younger by tightening the skin. As for implants, Dr. Tornambe cautions men to be aware of their tendency to shift after surgery. "Some gay men augment their bodies with calf, buttocks, and pectoral implants, but I have seen disasters." Once again, you should find a surgeon who has a great deal of experience in this area.

CHAPTER 14

Sexual Compulsivity, Hate Crimes, and Domestic Violence

SEXUAL COMPULSIVITY

Sexual compulsive behavior, like most addictions, involves an intense preoccupation with sexual activity that interferes with everyday living. Reggie, a fifty-six-year-old man born to alcohol-dependent parents, developed a strong urge to have sex with other men while still married to his wife. After their divorce he entered into a relationship with a man, but secretly engaged in sexual activity with other men. This behavior became compulsive. While trying to maintain his successful career, Reggie spent hours online trying to meet men in order to have sex. His behavior spun out of control, and as a result his work and his relationship suffered. It wasn't until his multiple affairs had come to light and his partner threatened to leave that he decided, for the sake of his relationship, to get help.

For some gay men, using sex can be a way to deal with internalized homophobia. For others, it is a means to fill the void or hole they feel in their lives. Growing up in an environment that portrays homosexuality as sinful or abnormal can lead to a distorted view of gay sex. Sometimes gay men take on multiple sex partners to avoid intimacy. Using men just for sex allows them to satisfy their lustful urges without feeling love because on some level they don't feel they deserve it. The result is a short-term relief often followed by shame and depression.

The desire to have sex as a form of escapism or pleasure is not unusual; however, for the compulsive, there is a psychological disconnection between the underlying issue and the physical need to fill the void. Sometimes this can manifest itself when men engage in frequent receptive anal sex as a way to physically fill their hole. Once again this misinterpreted response to a feeling of emptiness will only provide temporary relief followed by sadness.

In many ways, the nature of sexual compulsive behavior leads to more sex, sometimes with men who are abusive or unattractive. This perpetuates the cycle because afterwards there is guilt over what they have done. Half-hearted attempts at curtailing this behavior result in failure, and this is the *sin qua non* of the compulsive. More often then not, the sexual addict is not fully aware of his behavior and how it is affecting his life.

In addition to being consumed with sex, compulsives may engage in excessive masturbation, averaging six to eight orgasms a day. Some men have confessed to masturbating even while at work. Frequently, they utilize pornographic material in conjunction with masturbation. Many spend hours at home masturbating to pornographic movies while online trying to hook up. Others stay up all night high on crystal methamphetamine while engaging in anonymous sex. Then unable to work the next day, they spend that time sleeping and sinking into depression.

Many experts concur that sexual compulsive behavior is the result of an underlying psychological disorder. The sexual response is a maladaptive coping mechanism for depression and anxiety. Usually it affects men who come from dysfunctional families, while others report a history of sexual abuse. These experiences, in addition to growing up closeted, can develop into an intense sexual response. Gay children, in particular, develop a precocious pattern, especially in response to bullies and molesters. Later, they seek out men who have the same physical attributes and emotional characteristics of their abusers.

Ultimately, the concern is that the compulsive behavior will progress to the point where there is a total lack of control. This could eventually lead to loss of job or an end to a relationship. It is also quite common for sexual compulsives to engage in activity with other compulsives under the influence of alcohol and drugs. Certainly for gay men, recreational drugs, especially crystal meth and GHB, have facilitated excessive sexual behavior. The increased rates of HIV and syphilis are attributed to them. Frequently attending sex clubs and hiring sex workers is also commonplace, and the result is an increase in risky sexual behavior (Amico 1997).

Treatment for sexual compulsive behavior should include behavior therapy, either individual or group. Sexual Compulsives Anonymous (SCA) is similar to A.A.'s twelve-step program and includes the essentials for recovery:

> *Awareness of the disease*
> *Commitment to change*
> *The ability to surrender control*
> *Willingness to learn from those in recovery*

In some cases, medication, like serotonin re-uptake inhibitors (SSRIs), which include such brand-names as Prozac (fluoxetine), Zoloft (sertraline), and Paxil (paroxetine), have been used to treat the underlying depression or anxiety. Also, the side effects of these medications can include loss of libido, which can be beneficial for these men.

HATE CRIMES

In the summer of 2000, Joe and Tom were leaving New York's Gay Pride Pier Dance and began walking toward the West Village. Joe was struck from behind with a pipe and fell to the ground while his boyfriend charged at the assailants. Fortunately, Joe did not lose consciousness, but he sustained a mild concussion and a scalp laceration. Tom brought him to the hospital where he was treated and later sent home.

Years later, Joe continued to have episodes of severe anxiety, especially while walking the streets of Manhattan. He felt as if he had to look over his shoulder constantly, and he was uncomfortable with anyone walking too close behind him. Subsequently, Joe suffered from intense nightmares, and it wasn't until he discussed his symptoms with his doctor that he was diagnosed with post-traumatic stress disorder.

In the United States, 15 percent of all single-bias attacks were based on sexual orientation. The FBI reported in 2004 that the majority of those victims, 60.9 percent, were the object of anti–male homosexual attitudes. In light of these statistics, it is important to remember that gay bashing has been documented throughout history. Homosexuality was punishable by death even as far back as the Roman empire. Presently there are still countries, especially in the Muslim world, that punish homosexuality by death. However, even in this country, hate crimes against homosexuals are common. The most highly publicized was the beating death of Matthew Shepard in 1998, but these attacks occur daily. In a recent less-publicized incident, six men were brutally beaten in San Diego after their Gay Pride festival. The youngest attacker was just fifteen years old.

It is so important for gay men to treat these hateful attacks seriously. Some men feel ashamed afterward, and this can deter them from calling the police. Often gay men feel embarrassed and refuse to report such attacks to the police, fearing that they will not be sensitive. Anti-gay attitudes are a reality, but reporting these crimes is essential. For one, it gives the victim a sense of validity that these offenses should not happen. Also, for statistical purposes: The numbers are compiled in annual FBI reports and support political legislation against these crimes. Remember that it was only in 2003 that the Supreme Court overturned anti-sodomy—that is, gay sex—laws in fifty states.

Victims of hate crimes should be alert to symptoms consistent with post -traumatic stress disorder (PSTD), which is anxiety associated with experiencing or witnessing a physically or psychologically violent event. Signs to look for include flashback or nightmares, anger, exaggerated startle response, and intense reactions to situations that remind you of the event. Treatment for PSTD is focused on behavioral therapy, sometimes in conjunction with medication. SSRIs are often prescribed for this disorder because they alleviate the underlying depression and help with the anxiety. Long-term statistics show that gay men respond well to behavioral therapy, where they develop a sense of mastery over the anxiety.

DOMESTIC VIOLENCE

Abusive relationships involve one partner's attempt to physically or psychologically dominate the other. Nearly, one out of four gay relationships is abusive—roughly the same percentage as in heterosexual couples. Approximately one-third of the cases are reported. Until recently, attention to domestic violence in gay couples has been overlooked. Some have made the incorrect assumption that just because violence erupts in same-sex relationships, it is not abusive because the members of the couple are the same sex and therefore equally matched. Another reason that there is a scarcity of information includes the reluctance of some gay men to report such incidents to the police, fearing homophobia or insensitivity (Island and Letellier, 1991).

The CDC reported that 800,000 men per year are

raped or assaulted by their partner. It is estimated that over 300,000 men are stalked every year, and in 2002 it was revealed that 24 percent of male homicide victims were killed by their intimate partners.

Violence toward gay men by their partner includes not only physical violence but also sexual and emotional abuse. For some it involves intimidation or the threat of violence. Some abusers even enforce economic deprivation as a way to control their partner.

It is understood that most gay abusers suffer from low self-esteem or feelings of inadequacy due to internalized homophobia, while others harbor unresolved childhood conflicts. There are also genetic tendencies as well as psychosocial issues that come into play, like substance abuse, mental illness, and poverty. In any case hostility or resentment toward gay men compounded by internalized homophobia is another form of misandry, and should not be tolerated.

Roger was in a relationship with Kyle for nearly five years. After they broke up, Roger described this union as "toxic." Fueled by jealousy and resentment, these two carried out violent acts toward each other for years. One Sunday afternoon, Kyle paged his doctor and revealed that, after an exhausting night of drinking, he and Roger had gotten into a heated argument. In the end, Roger pulled a knife but, in his excitement, stabbed himself in the thigh. This case is a form of mutually exclusive abuse. Their cycle is propelled by co-dependency. After the "Acute Incident," they reorganized and progressed into the "Honeymoon Phase," which is characterized by affection and apology. Roger was lying on the couch with a towel wrapped in ice on his thigh, while Kyle attended to him.

Dr. Lenore Walker described this cycle of violence in her book *The Battered Woman*, based on interviews with

many women involved in abusive relationships. The model
of abuse consists of three distinct phases:

> *Phase 1: Tension Building: The couple builds
> up tension to the point where an argument
> develops.*
> *Phase 2: The Acute Incident: This is the actual
> fight.*
> *Phase 3: The Honeymoon Phase: The abuser
> apologizes for his actions and usually promises
> that it will never happen again. The couple
> experiences a renewed sense of love. This phase
> will slowly transform into the tension-building
> phase, and then the cycle will repeat itself.*

Walker points out that although the Honeymoon
Phase marks an end to the fighting with overcompensat-
ing affection, it only perpetuates the cycle of abuse. Some
gay men engage in submission and domination (S&M) as
a form of sexual role-play, allowing one of them to be de-
humanized or enslaved as a form of authoritarianism.
This is an exception to the definition of domestic violence, unless it is nonconsensual.

Other cases that involve consensual violence concern
men who enjoy being punched and choked during sex.
Some of the more graphic forms of pornography show violence as part of gay eroticism. Violence mixed in with
humiliation is perceived as sexy by some gay men.

Aside from the world of S&M, being victimized by
your partner does not stop on its own. Sometimes the
episodes can progress in frequency and severity. If you
feel you are being victimized, it is important to talk to
someone you can trust—and not your partner. Breaking
the silence is the first step in ending the cycle of abuse.

When you decide to leave, it is recommended that you have a safety plan. This should include having a trusted friend help you while you find a safe place to stay. Collect your money, clothes, and leave quickly. There are outreach programs geared toward the gay community. One in particular is the Gay Men's Domestic Violence Project at 1-800-832-1901. All counselors at the project are highly knowledgeable about any concerns you might have.

The bottom line is that no one deserves to be abused. It is important to remember that abuse comes in many different forms and that it is cyclical. The outcome of abuse is control, and the abused partner is rendered alone, isolated, and afraid. You should never feel that your actions warrant violence. Abuse is never your fault.

References

BOOKS

Anderson, Arnold E., ed. (1990) *Males with Eating Disorders.* New York: Brunner/Mazel.

Christensen, John B., Ira Telford (1988) *Synopsis of Gross Anatomy.* Philadelphia: J. B. Lippincott.

Gebjard, P. H., A. B. Johnson (1979) *The Kinsey Data: Marginal Tabulations of the 1938–1963 Interviews Conducted by the Institute for Sex Research.* Philadelphia: W. B. Saunders.

Goldstone, Stephen, M.D. (1999) *The Ins and Outs of Gay Sex.* New York: Dell Publishing.

Hall, Marny (1985) *The Lavender Couch: A Consumer's Guide to Psychotherapy for Lesbians and Gay Men.* Boston: Alyson Publications.

Holleran, Andrew (1986) *Dancer from the Dance*. New York: Penguin Books.

Island, D., and Letelliee, P. (1991) *Men Who Beat the Men Who Love Them: Battered Gay Men and Domestic Violence*. New York: Hawthorne Press.

Laumann, E. O., J. H. Gagnon, R. T. Michael, and S. Michaels (1994) *The Social Organization of Sexuality*. Chicago: University of Chicago Press.

Lee, Steven (2006) *Overcoming Crystal Meth Addiction*. New York: Marlowe and Co.

Michael, R. T., J. H. Gagnon, E. O. Laumann, and G. Kolata (1994) *Sex in America*. New York: Little, Brown.

Mooney, Michael, Nelson Vergel (2003) *Built to Survive: A Comprehensive Guide to the Medical Use of Anabolic Therapies, Nutrition, Supplementation and Exericise for HIV (+) Men and Women*. Program for Wellness Restoration Power.

Morin, Jack, Ph.D. (1998) *Anal Pleasure and Health*. San Francisco: Down There Press.

Penn, Robert E. (1997) *The Gay Men's Guide to Wellness: The National Gay and Lesbian Health Association's Complete Book of Physical, Emotional, and Mental Health and Well-Being for Every Gay Male*. New York: Henry Holt and Company.

Perricone, Nicholas, M.D. (2006) *Dr. Perricone's 7 Secrets to Beauty, Health, and Longevity: The Miracle of Cellular Rejuvenation*. New York: Ballantine Books.

Phillips, Bill (1999) *Body for Life*. New York: HarperCollins.

Sax, Paul E., M.D., Calvin J. Cohen, M.D., M.S., and Daniel R. Kuritzkes, M.D. (2007) *HIV Essentials*. Michigan: Physician's Press.

Shippen, Eugene, M.D., William Fryer (1998) *The Testosterone Syndrome*. New York: M. Evans and Company, Inc.

Signorile, Michelangelo (1997) *Life Outside: The Signorile Report on Gay Men: Sex, Drugs, Muscles, and the Passages of Life.* New York: HarperCollins.

Silverstein, Charles, M.D., Felice Picano (1992) *The New Joy of Gay Sex.* New York: HarperCollins.

Townsend, Larry (1996) *The Leatherman's Handbook II.* New York: Carlyle Communications.

Weiss, Robert (2005) *Cruise Control: Understanding Sex Addiction in Gay Men.* New York: Alyson Publications.

Wolfe, Daniel (2000) *Men Like Us: The GMHC Complete Guide to Gay Men's Sexual, Physical, and Emotional Well-Being.* New York: Ballantine Books.

Yudko, Errol, Harold V. Hall, and Sandra B. McPherson (2003) *Methamphetamine Use: Clinical and Forensic Aspects.* Florida: CRC Press.

Walker, Lenore (1979) *The Battered Woman.* New York: HarperCollins.

PERIODICALS

Adam, David. "Truth about Ecstasy's Unlikely Trip from Lab to Dance Floor: Pharmaceutical Company Unravels Drug's Chequered Past," *Guardian Unlimited,* August 18, 2006.

Amico, Joseph M. "Assessing Sexual Compulsivity and Addiction in Chemically Dependent Gay Men," *The Journal of Treatment and Prevention.* 1997; 4(4) 291–297.

Armstrong, G. L., A. Wasley, E. P. Simard, et al. "The Prevalence of Hepatitis C Virus Infection in the United States, 1999–2002," *Annals of Internal Medicine.* 2006; 144: 705–714.

Bancroft, J., Janssen, E., Strong, D., Carnes, L., Vukadinovic, Z., and Long, J.S. "Sexual Risk-Taking in Gay Men: The Relevance of Sexual Arousability, Mood and Sensation Seeking," *Archives of Sexual Behavior.* 32, 555–572.

Barrett, F. F., R. F. McGhee, and M. Finland: "Methicillin-Resistant *Staphylococcus aureus* at Boston City Hospital," *New England Journal of Medicine.* 1968; 279: 448.

Bates, K. L. "Study Fails to Find Link Between Marijuana Use and Cancer," *The University Record* Online, University of Michigan. October 16, 2006.

Bonanno, F. "Ketamine in War/Tropical Surgery (A Final Tribute to the Racemic Mixture)," *Injury,* 2002; 33 (4): 323-327.

Borlaug, C.I.C., M.P.H., Gwen, Davis, M.D., Jeffrey P., Fox, M.D., Barry C. (2005) "Guidelines for Clinical Management and Control of Transmission: Community Associated Methicillin-resistant *Staphylococcus aureus*" (Wisconsin Department of Health and Family Services), Centers for Disease Control and Prevention. "Hepatitis B Vaccination Coverage Among Adults: United States, 2004," *Morbidity and Mortality Weekly Report.* 2006; 55: 59–511.

Centers for Disease Control and Prevention. "Four Pediatric Deaths from Community Acquired Methicillin-resistant *Staphylococcus aureus*: Minnesota and North Dakota, 1997–1999," *Morbidity and Mortality Weekly Report.* 1999; 48: 707–710.

Centers for Disease Control and Prevention. "Sexually Transmitted Diseases: Guidelines 2002," *Morbidity and Mortality Weekly Report.* 2002; 51(RR-6): 18–29. Available at http://www.cdc.gov/std/treatment/default.htm

DeNavas, Walt C., B. Proctor, and C. H. Lee. "Income, Poverty, and Health Insurance Coverage in the United States: 2004." U.S. Census Bureau. August 2005.

Echavez, Michael, M.D., William Horstman, Ph.D. "Relationship Between Lipoatrophy and Quality of Life," *The AIDS Reader,* 2005; Vol. 15, No. 7: 369–374.

Goldie, S. J., K. M. Kuntz, M. C. Weinstein, et al. "The Clinical Effectiveness and Cost Effectiveness of Screening for Anal Squamous Intraepithelial Lesions in Homosexual and Bisexual HIV-Positive Men. *Journal of American Medical Association.* 1999; 281: 1822–1829.

Goldstone, Stephen E., M.D., Adam Kawalek, M.D., Jeff W. Huyett, M.S., A.P.R.N., B.C. "Infrared Goagularor: Useful Tool for Treating Anal Squamous Intraepithelial Lesions," *Diseases of the Colon and Rectum.* Vol. 48, No. 5, 1042–1054.

Hashibe, M., H. Morgenstern, Y. Cui, D. P. Tashkin, Z.-F. Zhang, W. Cozen, T. M. Lee, Nolan E., Melanie M. Taylor, Elizabeth Bancroft, Peter J. Morgan, Margie McCoy Lucie, and Paul A., Simon, "Risk Factors for Community-Associated Methicillin-Resistant *Staphylococcus aureus* Skin Infections among HIV-Positive Men Who Have Sex with Men," *Clinical Infectious Diseases.* 2005; 40: 1529–34.

Institute of Medicine. *Insuring America's Health: Principles and Recommendations.* The National Academies Press, 2004.

Institute of Medicine. *Care Without Coverage—Too Little, Too Late.* The National Academies Press, 2002.

Jaffe, H., et al. 14th CROI, Los Angeles. 2007; No. 63.

Klamen. "Smearing the Queer: Medical Bias in the Health Care of Gay Men," *JAMA.* 2000; 284: 1986–1987.

Kwong, J., K. Mayer, N. Peterson, et al. "Non-Occupational Post-Exposure Prophylaxis (PEP) at a Boston Community Health Center," The XIII International AIDS Conference, Durban, South Africa. 2000.

Landon, M. G., et al. "Outbreak of Boils in an Alaskan Village: A Case-Control Study," *Western Journal of Medicine.* 2000; 172: 235–39.

McCaig, Linda F., L. Clifford McDonald, Sanjay Mandal, and Daniel B. Jernigan, *"Staphylococcus aureus—* Associated Skin and Soft Tissue Infections in Ambulatory Care,"* Centers for Disease Control and Prevention, *E.I.D. Journal Home.* November 2006; Vol. 12, No. 11.

Mack, and S. Greenland. "Marijuana Use and the Risk of Lung and Upper Aerodigestive Cancers: Results of a Population-Based Case-Controlled Study," *Cancer Epidemiology, Biomarkers and Prevention,* 2006; Vol. 15, No. 10: 1829–1834.

Makadon, M.D., Harvey J., Kenneth H. Mayer, M.D., and Robert Garofalo, M.D., M.PH., "Optimizing Primary Care for Men Who Have Sex with Men," *Journal of American Medical Association.* 2006; Vol. 296, No. 19.

Manangan, L. P., and W. R. Jarvis. "Prevention of Methicillin-resistant *Staphylococcus aureus* (MRSA), Methicillin-Resistant *Staphylococcus epidermis* (MRSE), and Vancomycin-Resistant *Enteroccci* (VRE) Colonization/Infection," *Antibiotics for Clinicians.* 1998; 2:33–38.

Olney, J., J. Labruyere, and M. Price. "Pathological Changes Induced in Cerebrocortical Neurons by Phencyclidine and Related Drugs," *Science.* 1989; 244 (4910): 1360–2.

Osbourne, Duncan. "Resistant Staph Spreads among NYC Gay Men," *Gay City News.* 2007.

Rhoden, E.L., A. Morgentaler. "Medical Progress: Risks of Testosterone-Replacement Therapy and Recommendations for Monitoring," *New England Journal of Medicine* (2004); Vol. 350, No. 5.

Shalender, Bhasin, R. Glenn Cunningham, Frances J. Hayes, Alvin M. Matsumoto, Peter J. Snyder, Ronald S. Swerdloff, and Victor Montori. "Androgen Deficiency Syndromes in Men: Guideline Task Force," *Journal of Clinical Endocrinology and Metabolism* 2006; Vol. 91, Issue 6, 1995-2010.

Shalender, Bhasin, et al. "The Effects of Testosterone Supplementation on Whole Body and Regional Fat Mass and Distribution in Human Immunodeficiency Virus-Infected Men with Abdominal Obesity," *Journal of Clinical Endocrinology and Metabolism*. 2007; Vol. 92, No. 3, 1049-1057.

Slavin, S. "Recreational Use of Amyl Nitrite." *Venerology: The Interdisciplinary International Journal of Sexual Health*, 2001; 14 (2): 81–82.

"Twinrix Hepatitis A Inactived and Hepatitis B (Recombinant) Vaccine," *Physician's Desk Reference*. Montvale, NJ: Thomson O.DR. 2003; 1669–1672.

Van Griensven, F., et al. 14th CROI, Los Angeles. 2007; No. 55.

Zuardi, Antonio Waldo. "History of Cannabis as a Medicine: A Review," *Revista Brasileira de Psiquiatria*. 2006; 28(2): 153–157.

WEBSITES

http://www.gaycitynews.com/site/news.cfm?newsid= 17855835&BRD=2729&PAG=461&dept_id=568864&rfi

http://www.thebody.com/step/ezine_123003/mrsa_vre .html#

http://www.thebody.com/hepp/julaug04/spotlight.html

"Staph Infections Linked to 'Manscaping'" Study: Body shavers six . . .

www.sovo.com/2004/11-19/news/national/staph.cfm—18k

gaylife.about.com/cs/healthfitness/a/bodyimage.htm

http://www.cdc.gov/hiv/topics/surveillance/resources/ reports/2005report

www.myspace.com/FrankSpinelliMD

Index